The TAO of
RESEARCH

This book is dedicated to Thomas Albert Casadevall, father to Mary Lou and Dana's father-in-law. His life stands as a shining example of how one man can influence so many lives in such a positive way. Thank you, Tom.

The TAO of
RESEARCH
A Path to Validity

Dana K. Keller / Mary Lou Casadevall-Keller
Halcyon Research, Inc.

Los Angeles | London | New Delhi
Singapore | Washington DC

For information:

 SAGE Publications, Inc.
2455 Teller Road
Thousand Oaks, California 91320
E-mail: order@sagepub.com

SAGE Publications India Pvt. Ltd.
B 1/I 1 Mohan Cooperative
    Industrial Area
Mathura Road, New Delhi 110 044
India

SAGE Publications Ltd.
1 Oliver's Yard
55 City Road
London EC1Y 1SP
United Kingdom

SAGE Publications Asia-Pacific
    Pte. Ltd.
33 Pekin Street #02-01
Far East Square
Singapore 048763

Printed in the United States of America.

Library of Congress Cataloging-in-Publication Data

Keller, Dana K.
The tao of research: A path to validity/Dana K. Keller, Mary Lou Casadevall-Keller.
    p. cm.
ISBN 978-1-4129-6468-5 (pbk.: alk. paper)
    1. Research—Methodology. I. Casadevall-Keller, Mary Lou. II. Title.

Q180.55.M4K445 2010
001.4′2—dc22   2009002836

Printed on acid-free paper.

09   10   11   12   13   10   9   8   7   6   5   4   3   2   1

Acquiring Editor:	Vicki Knight
Associate Editor:	Sean Connelly
Editorial Assistant:	Lauren Habib
Production Editor:	Sarah K. Quesenberry
Copy Editor:	Liann Lech
Proofreader:	Wendy Jo Dymond
Typesetter:	C&M Digitals (P) Ltd.
Cover Designer:	Candice Harman
Marketing Manager:	Stephanie Adams

Contents

About the Authors

Dana K. Keller received his PhD in Measurement, Statistics, and Evaluation from the University of Delaware. As a professor, he supervised the research for more than 100 doctoral dissertations. As chief statistician for a $30 million nonprofit foundation, he was influential in establishing and implementing state and federal policies. He has explained research methodology, how it can be used, how it is often misused, and how to place it in its proper context throughout the United States and in places as far-reaching as Tibet. His informal presentation style facilitates a comfortable understanding of research in its appropriately restricted context. Dr. Keller can be reached at dana@halcyonresearch.com.

Mary Lou Casadevall-Keller received her MS in microbiology from the University of Delaware, as well as a BA in sociology and a BS in plant science. She embarked on a long career in corporate research, producing dozens of comprehensive market and product research reports, as well as a patent for a waterproof orthopedic cast liner. After corporate life, she worked to secure and monitor grants for community colleges and nonprofit organizations. She and her husband, Dr. Dana Keller, are currently co-owners of a health care research consulting firm, Halcyon Research, Inc.

Both authors are independent consultants.

Preface

Have you ever noticed that research findings can sound quite definitive and then be startlingly short-lived as facts? Did you ever wonder why? *The Tao of Research: A Path to Validity* explains the ways by which research is a human activity that regularly succumbs to human failings. Without untoward motivations, simple mistakes, lack of the right knowledge, impediments to the research, or an unconscious bias often result in wrong "knowledge" becoming part of shared cultural beliefs that can persist for years. Eventually, enough observations contradict those beliefs and prompt a reexamination of the evidence. The process by which we uncover evidence and then, through a context, turn that evidence into new knowledge is called research.

Research—the word itself puts us on the path to understanding its mission and its methods. Say it slowly . . . re-search. Research is looking again, trying once more to find something that was not found before. At a fundamental level, it is a search for truth, and nothing is harder to find or more tenuous to hold.

Although sometimes difficult to accept, knowledge in human terms is composed of both fact (the truth component) and supposition (guesses that fill in the gaps) because of the methods by which our brains process information. Sometimes, the supposition component is so small as to be trivial and can be rightfully ignored. Yet the notion that our knowledge is truth simply breaks down when examined very closely. Faulty or incomplete knowledge, plus unknown prejudices (from society's pervasive conditioning beyond our awareness), predestines a most human condition whereby the part of what we know that is supposition allows the rest of what we know to make sense to us. In other words, faulty yet often-accepted "knowledge," plus our unknown prejudices, yields what we truly believe is a complete understanding, when it simply is not. Notice that the uniquely individual aspect of filling in the gaps is what allows knowledge to make sense to each of us, separately. To the extent that supposition is minimized, our knowledge is more enduring, useful, and universal because it is closer to the truth.

Adhering to research principles makes our results more useful because the results do not depend as much on the unique conditions and assumptions under which they arose. The path of research approaches knowledge by safeguarding its factual component and minimizing the suppositional component in fundamental ways. This approach sets landmarks that most good research must pass on the path to knowledge creation. By minimizing supposition, validity (i.e., the truthful component of knowledge in the sense of contextual correctness or accuracy) is better assured.

Minimizing supposition is far easier said than done. The reason is that validity (i.e., appropriateness for a given purpose) involves judgment. In real-life research, results tend not to be as strong as researchers would prefer to see them. With only a modest strength to their evidence, even small flaws in research methodology can substantively alter results and our new knowledge. Even seemingly innocent choices in sampling or statistical techniques can have ramifications that find their way into "common knowledge" and then into policies that affect people's lives.

Just as with memories and judgment, the sufficiency continuum that we know as validity varies from person to person. Functionally, validity can be both arbitrary in the way it is implemented and arrogant in the way it is presented. Validity has an arbitrary component because it is often based on unrecognized suppositions. It can seem arrogant in that it too often considers its results as truth, rather than converging on more accurate knowledge. Whether in physical or social science, new evidence that contains proportionally larger factual components can overturn widely held and long-term beliefs that at the time were known simply as truths.

This book approaches the topic of research through an exploration of the issues that threaten validity in the process of knowledge generation. The strengths and weaknesses of research from a wide range of disciplines become clearer through an understanding of some basic principles through which science tries to minimize supposition and thereby maximize fact. This process is commonly known as ensuring validity. It would be more correctly called ensuring sufficient validity for a given purpose. Throughout the book, readers will notice facets of validity that might seem to be the hidden secrets of research, its version of skeletons in the closet—perhaps rightfully so.

As we traverse the landscape of research, we will be assisted by three guides. Readers familiar with *The Tao of Statistics: A Path to Understanding (With No Math)* (2006) will already be familiar with two of them, their questions, and their data. One guide is a high school principal in a midsized town. The second guide is the director of public health for a mid-Atlantic state. The third guide is a professor of sociology at a small liberal arts college. We will see that the choice of professions is of little consequence to understanding the concepts presented in the book. The concepts span a vast array of research activities, types of questions, and policy-relevant issues. Nonetheless, we will see the ways by which the high school principal uses his knowledge of research to better understand his school's needs. The director of public health uses her knowledge of research to help maximize her department's impact on the neediest citizens in her state. The sociology professor uses her knowledge of research to deepen our understanding of human nature.

We will see that the guides need to understand each concept within the contexts of their own localized environments. They combine their topic knowledge and an accommodation of local conditions with knowledge of research methodology to refine their research problems to fit their specific needs. This process is the heart of research, and understanding its implications for generated knowledge is the heart of this book. As the book progresses, readers will see that a research perspective is useful in many aspects of life. It opens our eyes to the frailty of our knowledge, humbles us to accept its limits, and challenges us to learn just that small amount more that brings us closer to an actual truth.

Importantly, our quest for knowledge is not only restricted by our suppositions, but it also actually requires these restrictions because of the nature of conducting research. As we will see, these restrictions are propositional, ethical, structural, functional, and technical. This organizing structure assists in understanding how the various aspects of research unite to form an overarching perspective on generating new knowledge and assessing its worth. Just sit back in a comfortable chair, in a place where the world can pass you by, and let yourself be led through a world where knowledge is a commodity that is often aggressively pursued but eventually spoils. It is a world where humility and arrogance appear as two sides of the same coin, a world where we know that what we know is not exactly so.

In finding a balance, to know which parts are likely "not exactly so," let the Tao act as a guide. The Tao is an eastern philosophy that promotes compassion, moderation, and humility. These are important characteristics for ethical research that can and should beneficially coexist with Western scientific methods.

Acknowledgments

We would like to thank the members of the staff at SAGE for helping to bring this book to life, as well as the following reviewers for their contributions:

Susan E. Dutch, Westfield State College

Paul R. Swank, University of Texas Health Science Center at Houston

Holmes Finch, Ball State University

Charles A. Loftus, Arizona State University

We would also like to thank Margot Kinberg for her critique and supportive friendship throughout the years

Our children, Zachary and Jason, for their loving support of their nontraditional parents

Each other, for the willingness to truly value each other's point of view in the adventurous life that we have shared

1. The Proposition's Restrictions

Cardiff

To convey meaning

Context demands

The audience knows

And truly understands

Propositional restrictions refer to the characteristics of the problem being studied (i.e., the proposition) in combination with the characteristics of the available environment. These characteristics limit researchers' abilities to derive results that stand the test of time—and many other researchers working on the same or a similar topic. These limits exist because certain things can be done, and others cannot (e.g., see the section on human participants); and certain things are known, and others are not (i.e., researchers never seem to be able to acquire all of the data on their "wish list"). Even things that researchers believe they know are rarely known with certainty or optimal precision. The result is that "perfect research" is most often an oxymoron, as has been seen countless times through the conflicting results touted in the media. These conflicting results, especially when published in a peer-reviewed journal, are not often a sign of poor research. Rather, they are the natural consequence of propositional restrictions, along with other restrictions detailed in later chapters.

The restrictions covered in this chapter are as follows:

a. Questions: the research questions driving the project. Good questions can lead to good research, but poor questions seldom do.

b. Reliability: repeatability or consistency. Whether the issue is test results (e.g., medical, education, etc.) or supposedly the same data extracted from two sources or in two different ways, the results should be about the same. Two "identical" blood tests from different labs should yield the same results from a split blood sample, as should two different IQ tests. Notice, no mention is being made of being correct in any aspect of reliability—simply repeatability or consistency.

c. Validity: the extent to which the available data reflect the characteristics thought to be the ones being studied; the intersection of intent with process. Here is where correctness matters. Repeatability is not enough. Everyone can be wrong, as the history of science has shown.

d. Generalizability: the extent to which research results can be trusted to be accurate for a parent population from which samples were derived. When entire populations are used, generalizability is not a problem.

   e. Assumptions: the conditions that are believed to be true without specific evidence. Although inevitable, assumptions are often handled by simply listing them in the research report.

   f. Bias: generally, the unconscious prejudicing of the study through researchers' preconceptions or through methodological flaws in the research. Personal bias can be harder to overcome than methodological flaws because it tends to be less apparent to an independent reader.

   g. Confounds: the characteristics that might actually be responsible for the results but were not accommodated in the research. Confounds are a major contributor—some would say *the* major contributor—to research results being reversed or greatly modified over time.

The remaining sections in this chapter each discuss these propositional restrictions in turn and how they are accommodated by a high school principal, a director of public health at the state level, and a professor of sociology. Through the examples listed throughout these sections, it becomes clear that research, as it is conducted, is very different from what might be thought. It is most often confined to more limited and poorer quality information than would be optimal for lasting results. These issues set the stage for the fragility of results that is commonly the unspoken hallmark of research.

1a. Questions

Facts don't quite fit
Not sufficiently pat
A revised look
Might answer that

Good research questions are a hallmark of good research. The reason is simple: Research questions motivate and define practically all ensuing aspects of a research design. Good research questions have well-defined terms and are objective, concrete, and answerable within the available resources.

The high school principal wants to know the extent to which extracurricular activities have an impact on grades. His superintendent has asked that the expense for the activities be justified or else the activities might be eliminated from a budget that seems to shrink every year. Although the principal genuinely believes in the value of these activities, his belief alone will not be sufficient to ensure their continuation.

In designing his research, he first drafted his question as, "Do students taking extracurricular activities get higher grades?" Upon reflection, he noticed that different types of students are engaged in extracurricular activities, and even these types of students differ according to the activities. For example, students from poorer families often have to work after school and do not attend extracurricular activities at all. Students on the math team seem quite different from stagehands for a school play in their aptitude for math. Furthermore, few people would assume that participation in a school play would be as effective at increasing math grades as would a math club. A good research question should be able to accommodate these issues without becoming overly long or complicated.

The principal revised his question to ask, "Is the addition of academic extracurricular activities associated with increased grades in associated courses?" The question has become better by being more restricted, but differences in students who are able to avail themselves of the opportunity to become involved in the relevant extracurricular activities must still be accommodated. Furthermore, the research results must also be adjusted for the initial achievement of the students (i.e., before becoming involved in the extracurricular activities). Nonetheless, the research question has become better by becoming more restricted. More restrictions will be added as other aspects of research are addressed.

The director of public health wants to know if public clinics are providing a substantial portion of the childhood immunizations that do not appear in her data. Unlike private physicians, clinics are not required to publicly report childhood immunizations in the state, and the legislature is reluctant to change the law. The governor wants to know the extent to which a related public health epidemic is plausible, given the numbers of children without a record of being immunized.

In designing her research, she originally asked the question "Do clinics immunize children?" Upon reflection, she sees that the stated question suggests a "yes" or "no" answer as the result. She is really interested in the extent to which children are being immunized in clinics. Her question becomes a bit more complicated: "What percentage of the childhood population receives immunizations from clinics, which do not publicly report the information?"

The data for answering her revised question likely will be difficult to obtain. Because the clinics are not required to publicly report the information, it is likely kept (if at all) in a manner that would be burdensome to retrieve. Yet the precision required of the project would likely allow for other methods to suffice. For example, clinics do need to track expenses and inventory. By asking for copies of the immunization shipment receipts and current inventories, estimates of the numbers of children immunized could be calculated by the number of doses no longer in inventory. The estimates would be less precise where multiple doses per child are needed, but the overall pattern of findings would likely be sufficient for her purpose.

The professor wants to know if matrilineal cultures have more equal rights for women than patrilineal cultures. Her personal interests lie with two west African cultures, and although she has been unable to secure funding for fieldwork abroad, she has arranged instead to meet with groups of immigrants in a nearby major metropolitan area. She has reliable access to several representatives from both west African ethnic groups. Furthermore, she can eat dinner at home with her family most evenings, so she is not entirely displeased with the research restriction of her not being able to travel to Africa at this time. Her original question was, "Do matrilineal cultures have more equal rights than patrilineal cultures?" After discussions with her colleagues and an assessment of her resources, she modified her question to be, "Do west African matrilineal cultures currently have more equal rights than west African patrilineal cultures?" The term *equal rights* is somewhat vague, but it appears to be well understood by her subjects to mean equal rights under the law, as well as by a cultural respect that is demonstrated by courteous behavior toward women.

Matrilineal cultures vary widely in the importance placed on females, and it is possible that our researcher will need to narrow her methodology to case studies of the two specific cultures she is researching. Nonetheless, some of her participants seem knowledgeable about their neighboring cultures, and our researcher is hoping to draw the broadest defensible generalizations from her project. She is reasonably confident that she can answer her questions in a scholarly manner without more costly fieldwork in Africa, at least for now.

1b. Reliability

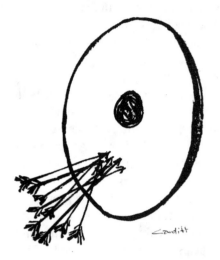

We all agree
Yet can be wrong
Reliability without validity
Is a very sad song

R eliability is the extent to which different methods or people would arrive at the same data or results. On the surface, it would seem to be a critical aspect of data and results—and it is—when the data and the results are sufficiently correct. Unfortunately, correctness is a characteristic of validity, not reliability. Therefore, although the common conception of reliability is somewhat over-rated, it forms the basis for validity, which is critical to good research. The reason is that validity cannot exist without reliability.

The question then becomes, "Why do researchers care about relia-bility?" The answer is that once something is repeatable, it is much easier to retarget or refocus than if it were not repeatable. For exam-ple, darts players first learn to throw darts with an identical motion time after time so the darts land in about the same spot on the board with practice (i.e., reliability). Only then do they shift where the darts will land (i.e., validity, when hit). Simply throwing darts at a board rarely results in a skilled player and most often serves to increase the randomness of the results (i.e., less reliability and validity).

The high school principal has two sources of data for achieve-ment, because the older hard copy system was recently replaced by an electronic system. His first thought is to test the extent to which grades were properly entered into the electronic system (i.e., the reliability of the electronic system). To compare the results of the two systems, the principal met with the district statistician to discuss sample size requirements. The sampling was conducted, grades were abstracted from the hard copy records, and a comparison was prepared. Much to the principal's surprise, only 97.8% of the grades matched. Some were off by more than a letter grade. Although 97.8% might sound like a high proportion (i.e., high reliability due to the high repeatability), the principal noted that it meant that approximately 264 grades were wrong in the population of grades, from a school with approximately 1,000 students. For most social science research, 97.8% reliability would be grounds for a celebration, but not for the principal. He had all of the hard copy grades checked, and those that did not agree were re-entered. A second check on the system revealed the reliability to be 99.7%, which the principal could accept.

The director of public health is willing to accept a far lower standard for reliability, in this case by necessity. The research requested by the governor does not need a precise answer and is really based on judgment coming from information that can be gathered. For example, her intended method for calculating doses of vaccine delivered to children (i.e., clinic receipts minus serum on hand) does not accurately account for some vaccines that require multiple doses. She knows from previous research that approximately 85% of children in her state who receive a single dose from a multiple protocol also receive the follow-up doses, so she can generate some estimates. Yet she also knows that vaccine sometimes expires without being used. Under that condition, state law requires the vaccine to be properly disposed of but does not require a record of the amount. The director of public health will also need to estimate clinic spoilage. These conditions require her acceptance of moderate reliability for the results—at best.

The professor has performed extensive reviews of historical documents on the subject, and she is conducting face-to-face interviews as well as observing the participants. She has arranged to live with two west African families, one matrilineal and one patrilineal, each for a week during her vacations. Qualitative research is often quite subjective, and even though she is attempting to be as objective as possible, she knows her small study may not be very reliable. She accommodates this by disclosing her restrictions and theoretical assumptions early in her writing. She also plans to focus on her personal interactions with each ethnic group, as she is an attractive young African American woman. The extent to which each group responds to her will be detailed in her findings.

1c. Validity

Certainty conferred

From a human source

Often proves false

When truth runs its course

In a very real sense, validity in research is the result of the intersection of our *intent* with the *process* of its implementation. Researchers believe that they know what they want to measure but often find that their available measures are somewhat compromised by being a blend of what they want to measure and something else. For example, when researchers want to know the impact of a certain drug on the course of a disease, they might be measuring not only the impact of the drug but also the impact of the potentially different lifestyle of people who would volunteer for a clinical trial, even when the volunteers are randomly divided into experimental and control groups. The reason is that the drug might work differently for the volunteers (who would be in a clinical trial and might also be changing their diets, exercising more, meditating, etc.) than for the general population. Random selection into experimental and control groups decreases this volunteer problem but does not eliminate it. The reason is that the drug might interact with one or more of the characteristics that are associated with being a volunteer.

For this example, the assumption is made that the drug is equally as effective as some unknown combination of volunteers' characteristics that (a) differ somewhat from the general population and (b) relieve the clinical condition under study. A second assumption is also made that both these unknown characteristics and the drug can only mitigate the symptoms to about the same degree. Under that assumption, researchers might find very little or no effect from the drug. Yet nonvolunteers (who do not have the critical volunteer characteristics) might have greatly benefited from the drug. The scenario might sound unlikely, but it is the unlikely scenarios that are less often explored, opening the door for compromised validity.

Can complete validity ever exist? Certainly, but complete validity generally requires a very restricted perspective. For example, the statement that a mummified body is dead would seem to be perfectly valid. Yet the statement assumes that the discussion is about the person who used to live in that body. There could still be copious amounts of living organisms within that body, meaning that the body is not completely devoid of life. The life that is still there could easily contaminate other experiments placed too close to the body. So, is it really dead?

Measurement theory combined with vast amounts of supporting literature also shows that perfect validity is a very elusive goal. For example, gender is often regarded as a variable that requires only two response categories to be completely valid: female and male—as evidenced by there being only two types of public restrooms (not including those labeled family or handicapped). Anatomists have long known that physical manifestations of gender form a continuum that is strongly bimodal at its limits (i.e., commonly accepted and mutually exclusive female or male traits), but that it is not insignificant between the typical examples that anchor the ends of the continuum. Intersex individuals (those with a blend of male and female characteristics) have been captured in art and sculpture for more than 1,000 years. If research involving gender ignores this issue, it is easy to see that the measure lacks perfect validity. How might the measure capture the full validity of the gender continuum? Simply adding a third category would suggest that all intersex individuals have substantively identical biological characteristics or features, which is also not true. The physical manifestations of gender form a continuum that lacks a perceived and well-accepted need for a scale. The result is that many intersex individuals feel disenfranchised when they must choose a restroom or are forced to choose between female and male to describe themselves. If this type of validity issue exists for a trait that is supposedly as easy to distinguish as gender and is very real for actual people, it becomes clearer why validity is an issue when assessing psychological or other less supposedly obvious traits or characteristics that often must be inferred, such as assessing academic knowledge from a relatively small sample of questions.

Physical sciences, such as physics, are not immune to the issue of compromised validity in measurement, as the Uncertainty Principle demonstrates. The very act of measuring something in the physical sciences has long been known to slightly alter the object of the measurement. The measurements might be very close to fully valid, but "close" is not perfect.

Ethnographic research, which often involves a holistic approach to validity through the simultaneous synthesis of many aspects of the issue under study, can be invisibly subject to the impact of pervasive conditioning. Pervasive conditioning is the process by which our lifelong experiences cause us to assume certain things are true when, in fact, they might not be. Pervasive conditioning exists because our experiences are perceptual. The observer, the act of observing, and the object of the observation become intertwined in fundamental ways—on purpose. Although this type of research often reaches conclusions with exemplary explanatory and predictive validity, it might not. For example, ethnographic researchers might want to explore the impact of psychological counseling on depression. Watching the process and seeing that many more patients are improving than not, the conclusion might be drawn that the counseling appeared to be an effective treatment modality. Yet if symptoms of depression tended to resolve themselves with time, counseling could actually be making the condition worse but invisibly so to the researchers. The patients' depression, overall, might possibly have resolved more quickly without treatment, but would the resolution have been as long lasting? Ethnographic research seeks to limit the impact of these types of issues through a long-standing awareness of them and efforts to mitigate them whenever possible.

Even the term *validity* is ambiguous because of the range of plausible research questions. For example, is a measure intended to explain the past, present, or future? Is a relationship between two measures viewed as circumstantial, causal, or both, mitigated by a third variable? Is the researcher seeking to generalize the results to a parent population, while acknowledging the difficulty in acquiring a truly representative sample from most large-scale populations?

On balance, three questions must be asked when assessing most forms of validity. First, to what extent is the measure (or the result) sufficiently valid for its intended purpose? Second, how well can the answer to the first question be evidenced? Third, is the risk of the results being plausibly wrong or potentially harming others worth the information that is provided by the research?

The third question forms the basis for appropriate self-censorship in research because of the inherently questionable aspects of a measure's validity. At some extent, in the continuum of validity, the research answers can become worse than useless; they can become harmful. For example, assume that researchers who were piloting a novel parenting method found that it resulted in children with not only increased adaptiveness but also an increased tendency toward aggression. The researchers might decide to withhold their results until they could disentangle the portion of the parenting method that was associated with increased adaptiveness from the portion associated with increased aggression. At that point, the revised method could be assessed. If the increased tendency toward aggression were greatly mitigated by the newer approach, the researchers might feel comfortable releasing news of the method, along with an appropriate warning on the still existing, but greatly lessened, aggressiveness issue. A more sobering probability is that the researchers seeking a parenting method that increased adaptiveness might not have also thought to test for increased aggressiveness.

Nonetheless, two aspects of validity become clear once it is understood that validity ultimately relies on logic or judgment, at least to some extent. First, there is an arbitrary nature to validity. One only has to examine the performances that were considered perfection in the diving competitions in the Olympic Games over the decades to see the evolving nature of a perfect score—the fully valid exhibition of the skill. Performances that took gold medals many years ago would often fail to qualify for a national team today. Why? Because the competitions' judges long ago did not believe that people were capable of safely performing some of today's more complicated maneuvers. Their pervasive conditioning led them to believe that the best that they saw was the best that existed—or perhaps could exist. The distinction is not always clear, but it speaks to the heart of validity. When is something exactly what it should be? How should it be compared with something else that is exactly as it should be but is much harder to do? In today's Olympic Games, the degree of difficulty for a dive is accommodated through its maximum allowable scoring, but a remnant of this issue still exists.

This remnant leads to the second aspect of validity that derives from it ultimately resting on logic or judgment—an appearance of arrogance that is associated with the authority to decide the extent to which a measurement (or Olympic performance) is valid. What makes someone qualified to pass judgment on validity or even to decide how it will be measured? How can any individual escape lifelong pervasive conditioning to be able to employ fully objective judgment? Is validity hopelessly confounded with temporal events? Is the nature of validity inexorably linked to one's environment and place in time? Should or can enduring validity be a special type of validity that is not necessary for some types of research? If so, for how long, and how do we know? Issues of reliability suddenly seem so simple by comparison to issues of validity, which can be quite humbling. In time, some researchers become somewhat cavalier to the difference. When they do, they often find that relaxed attitude to be a big mistake.

The principal knows that differences in student grades often involve a constellation of characteristics interacting with their environment. He knows that his question is not only simultaneously simplistic on its surface, but also far too complicated to support more than a tentative answer, regardless of the logic suggesting that academic clubs are designed to promote achievement in their subject matter. He knows that, although the association between club content and course content is logically sound and pedagogically defensible, his superintendent will want to see quantitative results in addition to qualitative reasoning.

In considering his approach, the principal further reflected on the nature of validity because it would have an impact on both his qualitative reasoning and research into the clubs' and courses' contents and interactions with students, along with his quantitative results. From a qualitative perspective, he understood that the clubs were developed with charters that specifically addressed course content. He saw students participating in club events that evidenced course content. Teachers stated that the students in the club increased their knowledge of specific course content more than students who did not participate in content-related clubs, if for no other reason than increased practice. The principal was fairly certain that his qualitative case was reasonably strong, despite the plausible caveats on the lack of independence among the observers and the events.

When the principal thought about the ways in which plausible issues with validity could affect his results, he reworded his research question a second time. His question was, "Is the addition of academic extracurricular activities associated with increased grades in associated courses?" It became, "To what extent does the addition of academic extracurricular activities appear to be associated with increased grades in associated courses?" Now the question more clearly implies not only the need for a quantitative answer, but it also suggests that his answer will fall along a continuum, rather than the yes/no answer previously implied. Furthermore, his new question also includes a sense that he might not be able to arrive at a definitive answer—a personal disposition that is more aligned with a research perspective and speaks to the somewhat elusive nature of validity.

The director of public health knows that she will have data with at least somewhat compromised validity. Issues involving multiple doses for many types of vaccines and the disposal of unused serum impose the need for the acceptance of more ambiguity in her results than for much of the other research that she has previously done. This ambiguity translates to decreased validity. She will need to decide if the amount of truth in her answer sufficiently outweighs the uncertainty in it to be justified. The validity of her results would be somewhat compromised by the uncertainty in her measures, but she feels that there is enough "truth" that she can capture to yield a reasonable answer. Therefore, she will appropriately qualify her report's results to reflect her perception of the degree of validity of her data and refer to that report if her results are ever taken out of context—a somewhat persistent concern for many people who write documents within the public domain, such as hers.

The professor's research is much more qualitative in nature compared to our other two researchers' projects. Although there is an abundance of data on the status of women in each culture, her question is intentionally vague enough to include input from her fieldwork. Nonetheless, the anecdotal information that she gathers will need to agree substantially with the facts garnered from the international data on education, employment, health, and laws. One key fact she had already found is that women own 50% of the land in the matrilineal culture she is studying, compared to 2% for the neighboring patrilineal culture, which is the second culture she will survey.

Her qualitative research is studying a slice in time and is concerned with topics that do not fit into preexisting categories. Validity is couched in terms of the many restrictions on the complexities inherent in human interactions. Her study participants believe that they are offering valid opinions and true reflections of their own experiences. Yet their own situations could distort their perceptions sufficiently to make a general statement of validity impossible to justify. The professor knows this and seeks to gather information from sources with varied backgrounds within each culture. She will be interviewing new immigrants with refugee status, as well as college professors and successful business owners. Her past research has taught her that she will be hearing very different stories from each group, and accommodating those will be a challenge.

1d. Generalizability

The importance of context
Cannot be overstated
For results to generalize
Situations must be related

The results of research are said to be generalizable when they apply to a larger group than was studied. For research results to be generalizable, one of two conditions must exist. First, the sample used for the study must be a sufficiently valid subset of the overall population, or, second and alternatively, the group to which the results are being generalized must be shown to be substantively equivalent to the studied population for all traits that could impact the topic of the study. Although deriving an appropriately representative sample is conceptually easier and most often the method employed, it is not devoid of threats to the validity of the generalizability.

An example often used is that of researchers who want to survey a sample from a town's population. How would it be done? Phone lists would not capture certain types of individuals who tend to have unlisted phone numbers. Property lists would not capture renters. Even a complete list of all residents in the town would miss homeless people. Such a list could also include units in hotels and motels—some of the residents of which are permanent, although many others are not.

At some level, the idea of completely generalizable research results often disintegrates. The task of researchers is to be both careful and thorough in their descriptions of the extent to which generalizing might be problematic for their results. This issue is at the heart of the sections of peer-reviewed journals that speak to the population, the sample description and sampling methodology, and some of the limitations that are discussed. Although many readers skim over the Limitations sections thinking that the issues are little more than technical verbiage, these sections spell out the extent to which the knowledge generated has been restricted by the various conditions under which that knowledge was generated.

The principal views his populations as relatively small, and his electronic records system has been tested for reliability with regard to student grades. Upon some reflection, the principal realized that agreement (i.e., repeatability) between the two sources of grades met the definition of reliability, but one of those sources was the permanent student record. The contents of that record are considered historical truth, even when records are recent. The principal realized that he had actually verified the validity of his electronic records systems when he had originally thought that only the reliability had been assessed. Then the principal remembered that only the validity of the students' grades had been validated and not any of the other information in the electronic record.

The principal now faces the choice of validating the other types of information that he will be using to try to adjust for the types of differences in students that could be related to both attendance at academic clubs and improved achievement in the related courses. If he validates the other types of information that he will be using, he will not need to use samples but could use all of his student data. Given that the impact of clubs might be relatively small, he wants all of the statistical *power* to find a difference, if one is there—which he knows comes with larger numbers of students in his study. An additional advantage is that generalizability is not an issue when the entire population is used, unless the principal wants to generalize over time to a future group of students.

The appropriateness of using a population as a sample in time to compare or predict results often draws a mixed response from both research methodologists and statisticians. Except for truly longitudinal studies, little, if anything, is generally done to show the comparability of the two populations over time that are being compared. Changes in the measures could be due, at least in part, to changes in the population, which is rarely the topic of a study. In short, statistics are designed to explore differences that involve samples, not populations. For that reason, many research methodologists are somewhat reluctant to design studies that use statistical reasoning with populations. Nonetheless, the use of populations across time as if they were samples in time is a staple of public health research. For public health, changes in the population do not change their goal of mitigating disease, especially through process changes that have an impact on entire populations.

The director of public health has the electronic records for every affected individual in her state. Although she could conduct much of her research with entire populations, she wants to examine the uncertainties surrounding multiple vaccine doses and disposal. To do so, she will need to examine the records from a sample of clinics. She understands that the sampling is not straightforward. She will have samples of both vaccine shipments/disposals and beneficiaries, both of which are contained within the processes and procedures of clinics (a situation called *nesting* in research). Further complicating her acquiring anything close to a random sample, some of the clinics are fully independent whereas others are part of a chain with shared practices. Trying quantitatively to understand dosing and disposal will require the assistance of the department's statistician for both the sampling and the proper aggregation of the resulting information (data become information when placed in a context).

The professor knows that her results will need all of their restrictions carefully noted in order for them to be generalizable. Nonetheless, her research is one small piece of the larger puzzle that is human nature. Some of the pieces already in this puzzle include well-accepted findings, such as the following: Women who attend school can be generalized to have more opportunities for employment than women who do not receive a formal education, and better employment can be generalized to increased access to health care and decreased exposure to dangerous living conditions. To the professor, understanding the role that tracing a lineage through the mother (instead of the father) plays in empowering women seems an interesting piece to the puzzle.

1e. Assumptions

A critical piece
To fill in the gaps
That unknown fault
Where mountains collapse

Assumptions can be (and often are) defined as the specific data and situational requirements for statistical and methodological techniques, respectively, to be valid. Statistical assumptions are listed in many statistics texts and are often liberally sprinkled with Greek letters. Although this category of assumptions is important, its handling is generally best left to statisticians and research methodologists when technical issues need consideration. The outcome of minor violations of statistical and methodological assumptions for many, if not most, studies is marginally biased results that do not invalidate the substantive findings of the research. The reason is that substantive knowledge from researchers in conjunction with review, oversight, and publishing requirements generally results in reasonably sound statistics and research methodology.

The bigger threat from assumptions for the validity of research stems from our unknown assumptions. These assumptions arise from a lifetime of experience with the way we interact with the world. For example, if a dozen or so American men were asked the number of outs in an inning of baseball, most odds-makers would suggest that at least a few of those men would be willing to wager their last dollar that they knew the correct answer. Yet in many parts of the world, the men would look at each other and ask if any of them knew what an "out" or an "inning" was. Knowledge, actions, reactions, and a host of other traits that might be expected of others could be the result of how we grew up and were conditioned—hence, the term *pervasive conditioning*.

Pervasive conditioning can mask true causes by affecting both the target of the study and whatever researchers believe is responsible for variation in it—and researchers could be definitionally unaware of it. Peer-review processes, international committees, and other structures have been established to try to limit the impact of this type of threat to the validity of research results. Yet the threat from pervasive conditioning for the validity of results can also serve to remind researchers to be somewhat humble with regard to those results. Again, being cavalier about the impact of pervasive conditioning on validity has caused many reputations to be damaged.

The high school principal knows that the conditions of students' self-selecting academic clubs and coming from backgrounds that do not require after-school employment violate the notion that he might be able to look at a random sample of his students. His findings need to be qualified only to apply to the types of students who were in the academic clubs. This part of his assumptions does not trouble him.

Yet the nesting of students within clubs is a difficult situation, both statistically and methodologically. If randomness cannot be assumed, many of the statistical and methodological techniques taught to undergraduates are not valid approaches without some type of special handling. Knowing when he does not know enough, the principal will discuss the various stages of his project with his district's statistician—also the district's research methodologist.

The director of public health will have few, if any, problems with the assumptions underlying the use of her electronic data. Those data are population based, have been used for many years, and are well understood. Nonetheless, her study of multiple dosing and disposal presents problems. The state's clinics are not independently owned and operated, so their processes and procedures are likely shared and cannot be considered as randomly selected examples. The assumption of independence in observations is central to many methods of sampling. Sampling under the condition of poorly characterized partial dependence will certainly motivate her to involve the district's statistician.

The professor has made assumptions based on her previous field-work to western Africa and her more recent review of the current situation. Her study participants have been specifically chosen to challenge these assumptions. She wants to hear all sides of the story. Her contacts with more affluent members of the ethnic groups have led her to believe that women who own land have more security and independence than those who are landless. By including new immi-grants in the study, many of whom came from dire circumstances, the professor hopes to challenge her own thoughts about land ownership.

The professor is working with new data, which were gathered by a highly credible international organization. The new report is much more complete than were previous reports, and it serves as the back-bone for the quantitative portion of her study. She has discussed her project with others in her department, and she consulted with the college's research center, where a research methodologist reviewed her proposal and found that it was sound. He advised her to continue to scan the current literature for similar articles, as it would not be due diligence to duplicate another person's research. Our professor hopes to publish her work and present her results at a national con-ference, and she recognizes the value of his advice.

1f. Bias

Our parents before us
Friends and culture, too
Color our vision
Twist our point of view

Just as for assumptions, two types of bias are often considered in research: personal bias and technical bias. Personal biases, generally from our pervasive conditioning, can substantively affect several aspects of complicated studies because the number of judgments and decisions can be enormous. These decisions, all of which are influenced by bias, can greatly influence a study's results. Most researchers and educated consumers of research understand the issue and use structural methods, such as random sampling, whenever possible to avoid many of these judgments and decisions. Limitations sections are often included with results to discuss plausible sources of bias, among other topics.

Technical bias exists when the chosen techniques systematically overstate or understate the "true" results. Many sources of technical bias have been well characterized, such as the misleading nature of using the arithmetic mean as the average of a population's income. In this example, extremely large incomes by relatively few individuals can make the average income appear functionally larger than it really is. An extreme case could be when one individual earns $10 billion, and 999,999 people earn nothing. The arithmetic mean suggests that a typical person in that group earns $10,000. Yet only one individual earns even one dime. Both the median (the point where half are lower and half are higher) and the mode (the most common occurrence) return $0 earnings for the typical person in that group, which is a functionally unbiased estimate of typical earnings compared with the arithmetic mean.

Fortunately, technical bias as a restriction on the basic propositions driving research has been well characterized for most situations, and appropriate techniques are generally employed to mitigate the effects. Nonetheless, examples reach the public with almost alarming frequency. Continuing the previous example, average salaries for various occupations are often presented in the media. Which average is being presented (i.e., mean, median, mode)? How variable are the presented amounts by experience and by geographical location? Who gathered and supplied the data, and might they have an alternative agenda? It quickly becomes clear that the absence of a detailed context results in little or no useful information. The reason is that data require a context to become relevant, and relevance is required for information to be useful.

The principal knows that the population of students in academic clubs is a biased sample of his entire student population. Nonetheless, he also knows that he can accommodate this source of bias by being careful with the strength and generalizability of his results. At best, he expects his results to tentatively support the hypothesis that increased academic gains are associated from club activities. But now he has an additional problem.

The principal just realized that he has very real expectations for his results before embarking on the study. Consciously or not, he knows that his objectivity might be compromised. For this reason, he asks his district methodologist for ongoing oversight as a method of ensuring an unbiased approach to the various stages of the project.

The director of public health does not foresee any problems with technical bias with regard to the portion of her work that used her electronic data. The clinic sampling and resulting data, however, require special statistical handling or would likely show biased results. Moreover, even with special handling, the results are likely to be somewhat biased in unknown ways because of the relative lack of current information on the extent to which ownership and policies overlap across clinics.

The professor acknowledges her personal and professional biases. After 10 years researching women's issues in west Africa, and with the addition of better statistics collected by international organizations, she feels that she knows her outcomes in advance. Nonetheless, she is trying to maintain a fresh perspective for this study and has included more men and a greater diversity of women than previous studies that she has read.

The situation where a researcher knows there might be biasing technical considerations that cannot be adequately rectified is all too common. This issue has resulted in the Limitations sections normally found in scholarly articles. Through the Limitations section, researchers delineate known and potential sources of bias for their results.

Personal bias is rarely, if ever, discussed in research results because personal bias has no legitimate place in research. Nonetheless, people design, conduct, and analyze the data research studies. The existence of pervasive conditioning alone argues for a more transparent approach to acknowledging and accommodating the issue, as was done by the principal.

1g. Confounds

Evidence confirms
It must be so
Heard later in the halls
We just didn't know

Confounds are the missing ingredients waiting to catch up with every researcher. A confound is a variable that is related to both the dependent variable (the variable of interest) and the independent variable of interest (an explanatory variable) but whose influence has not been ruled out or otherwise accommodated.

Three ways exist to accommodate potential confounds. The first and best method is through the research design, where a strong design mitigates against many common sources of confounds. The second method is through accommodating statistics, where the impact of these variables is mathematically controlled. The third and weakest approach is by appealing to logic and argument: the "it only makes sense that . . ." tactic.

Few journals accept the third technique. Most reputable information outlets (journals, books, national media, etc.) prefer the first method but also will accept strong examples of the second. Publishers know that confounds eventually surface, are resolved, and often overturn research results; so, they are particularly sensitive to research designs that are more prone to plausible confounds, such as those using a nonrandom sampling methodology.

In the end, though, researchers can neither think of nor control for everything that might be responsible for some of the findings that were ascribed to something else. To advance knowledge, researchers must be willing to risk being wrong, while trying hard to avoid it.

Importantly, it is often from showing where others were wrong that knowledge achieves its largest gains. The reason is that others are not restricted by their pervasive conditioning in the exact way that the original researcher was restricted. Because of the uniqueness of what each of us knows, combined with the differences in each of our pervasive conditionings, others can see our research mistakes more easily than we can see them. Knowing this cycle of iterative improvements on others' work, researchers are wise to remain some-what humble in the presentation of their results.

The principal realizes that the potential list of background and personal characteristics that could be associated with academic club participation could be enormous. The thought that he could control for all of them would be preposterous. Even if he knew exactly which variables would need statistical control and had the required data, he would not have a large enough sample for the basic calcula-tions. The reason is that the needed sample sizes increase rapidly when control variables are added to the equations. Understanding this issue alone is a sufficient reason to maintain a strictly tentative approach to the reported findings.

The director of public health knows that the issues of multiple doses and the lack of complete disposal documentation will make her results somewhat tentative. Yet her work will yield a better esti-mate of immunization coverage than has been previously available. Although she doubts that she will miss anything major, the issue of confounds often cannot be completely resolved in most research.

The professor is pleased with the new data, which she feels sup-port her hypothesis and add objectivity to her long-held belief that land ownership patterns associated with matrilineal cultures lead to more security and independence for women and their children. Nonetheless, with the complexity inherent in human nature, she anti-cipates that she will glean some new insights from her fieldwork that might present one or more confounds that she will need to accom-modate in some manner.

2. Ethical Restrictions

The ability and the right

Are not the same venue

Know the difference

So research can continue

S imply put, it is not acceptable to knowingly risk causing harm to individuals or groups when planning, conducting, documenting, or presenting the vast majority of research. Although a debate exists as to the extent to which the same principle also applies to other sentient beings, history suggests that erring on the side of overextending the principle will likely be more consistent with the future's view of the topic than would underextending it. Notably, some exceptions exist (e.g., forensic investigations), but these exceptions are rare.

The burden on researchers, by default, is to preserve the anonymity; safety (e.g., physical, mental, emotional, professional, economic); and dignity of their participants. A specialized and independent group, often called an Institutional Review Board (IRB), must review any activities that could plausibly compromise any of these issues before they are implemented. Nonetheless, the absence of an IRB or its equivalent does not release researchers from their do-no-harm responsibility. The extent to which the principle becomes generalized beyond people and many species of animals, however, often seems based more on economics and marketing than on ethics.

Racial profiling within law enforcement could serve as a prime example of a situation where the ability to use statistics to increase the probability of a successful police action does not justify its use. With racial profiling, the additional risk of unjustifiably detaining the profiled but innocent individuals cannot justify the likely concomitant increase in the rate of successful arrests. Putting the innocent at increased risk is not acceptable, including participants in research, whether it is through their personal involvement or by using data associated with them.

Environmental concerns are generally considered as more legalistic than ethical in their restrictive effect on the conduct of research. This situation must and will change. The path of research dictates that the do-no-harm approach must be extended to all sentient beings and then to the environment itself. Although the process of working through appropriate guidelines and policies can be time consuming and cumbersome, just having an evolving process available to all researchers would advance the ethical standing of research. If there truly are rights to conduct and to report the results from research, they should not conflict with the rights and respect due to people, animals, and the environment.

The restrictions covered in this chapter are as follows:

a. Human participants: issues surrounding the use of people, alive or dead, or their data.

b. Privacy: normally considered a component of human participants' considerations, the issues of personal, professional, and economic privacy can be enormous. As such, these issues are separately discussed.

c. Animal testing: ongoing science continues to document various types of intelligence in an ever more diverse range of species. The path of research should err on the side of compassion, both by intent and by design.

The remaining sections in this chapter each discuss these propositional restrictions in turn and how they are accommodated by the high school principal, the director of public health, and the sociology professor.

2a. Human Participants

The Golden Rule

Is one way to say

Treat subjects with respect

Keep ambitions at bay

Human wartime atrocities, many under the guise of research on humans' adaptability and survivability, cast a bright spotlight on the rights of humans being studied. In short, the knowledge gained cannot justify the methods used—a principle with widespread application along the path of research, as well as of life.

Informed consent plays a major role in the use of human participants. The specific issues involved are generally delineated by the funding source or local IRB. Nonetheless, the lack of a prescribed process does not relieve the researcher from following a generic process. For example, certain elements usually will be found in an informed consent document. Although many other elements might need to be added to accommodate the specifics of the planned research, as is generally the case with medical research, informed consent documents generally include the following:

a. The purposes of the study

b. Detailed description of the procedures directly involving human participants

c. Identification of any procedures that are experimental

d. Any foreseeable risks or discomforts to participants

e. The expected duration for participation

f. Voluntary participation in a research study

g. No penalty for refusal or withdrawal

h. Plausible benefits to participants or to others that might result

i. The extent to which confidentiality will be maintained, and the methods used

j. A point of contact for questions about the research and about participants' rights

As already mentioned, IRBs are becoming a traditional approach to safeguarding the rights of human participants. These committees should also safeguard the rights of graduate students and others who might be susceptible to being drafted into the conduct of the project. For example, if an experiment required constant monitoring for 36 hours and only one person was available for the task, the project should be placed on hold until appropriate monitoring shifts could be arranged. In short, all aspects of research are subject to maintaining appropriate human dignity and safe conditions. In this context, "safe" can and should be generalized to all aspects of human privacy and dignity as well.

The principal will be using student-level data, some of which are sensitive, such as access to subsidized meals at school. He will also be involving the district statistician and secretarial assistance first to prepare the data. All personnel involved, however, have security training and clearance at the appropriate levels. Furthermore, his reports will have data aggregated to a level that cannot identify any particular students. Nonetheless, specific faculty advisors could be identified if the clubs were mentioned by name. The principal recognizes that the rights of human participants, although often somewhat different for minors than for adults, apply to all people participating in the study—actively or passively. To resolve the issue, he will obtain informed consent from willing faculty advisors and either aggregate the clubs' results or assign sequential letter names (e.g., Club A) for a random listing of the involved clubs.

The director of public health can rely on the legal architecture engineered by the state for the use of public health data. Staff who must see sensitive information are trained in the proper handling, storage, and disposal techniques. Reports are always aggregated to anonymous levels or relabeled when necessary. She does not even need clearance to visit the state's clinics for her investigation of the vaccine use and disposal issues, as she is entitled to do so any time and without prior notice. Her reports are a matter of public record. In short, she sees no human participants' issues for her proposed study.

The professor has informed consent forms for every person she plans to interview, and she hopes to include personal stories in her writings and when presenting her findings. She plans to take video footage of many of the interviews to use in class and at conferences. Her training in ethics and natural respect for all people will guide her interviews.

2b. Privacy

Know of others with caution

Secrets cut like a knife

Once out in the open

They grow larger than life

*W*hen is something public, when is it private, and for whom? Can a picture taken from the street of a person's house be made public without written consent? Does it matter if anyone inside can be seen? Does it depend on the people's activities or the extent to which they are identifiable? The courts have their answer(s) to many such questions. Yet adherence to the letter of the law(s) is a necessary but not sufficient orientation for the path of research. Extend the spirit of the law to include all issues that might cause people (a wide range of different types of people) to become uncomfortable with the exposure. This issue is not one where a single, personal frame of reference is generally considered valid. This issue is sufficiently important to deserve special consideration, apart from ethics concerning human participants overall, for which it is certainly a component.

IRBs can greatly assist with ensuring privacy issues, but not only the privacy of participants. The issue of privacy extends to the funding institutions, research institution, and administration officials at potentially all levels. These concerns are privacy matters where researchers might be uninvolved and, therefore, unaware. Nonetheless, privacy is one of those issues where a soft voice usually tells people the right thing to do. Researchers need to listen for and to that voice. When in doubt, this area is one where it really is vital to err on the side of protectionism.

The high school principal did not originally think that privacy would be an issue for his data. He would be aggregating the results and not identifying any of the students. The teachers would be identifiable for both courses taught and clubs mentored, but that type of exposure would normally be expected as part of the job. Yet, upon reflection, the principal felt that positive results might serve as an added opportunity for the more academically successful students to taunt those less gifted or less able to participate in academic clubs (e.g., poorer students tend to need an after-school job). He resolves to share his results and privacy concerns only with the school board and the district superintendent. Overall, the principal believes that the privacy risks are not sufficiently great to stop the project.

The director of public health also believes that any privacy concerns are minor. For example, although she will be investigating the disposal of dated vaccine, the clinics are obligated to dispose of it. No regulations exist for the amount that is disposed, only the method of disposal. Furthermore, all of her person-level data will be aggregated such that no individuals could be identified. She postulates that the only people who might feel somewhat poorly about a negative report (she believes that everyone would like to see a positive outcome) are those who are charged with the responsibility for having the vaccine administered. This group includes parents or guardians and the associated primary health care personnel. If the report is negative, these are the people who should know and then take action to secure the appropriate immunizations for their children. Furthermore, school health offices are supposed to ensure appropriate immunizations for all children. If she shows that many children are not immunized, only one of two conditions can exist. First, either the data are bad or the responsible individuals need to have their children immunized. Given this situation, the director of public health sees no privacy issues at all.

The professor plans to discuss privacy with all of her participants at length. There are many reasons for a person to want to maintain anonymity, and they all need to be respected. Before appearing in a video that could be seen by hundreds of people and, with the Internet, possibly millions, a person should give careful consideration to the potential exposure. Anyone who does not want to appear on video would not have to, and the equipment does not come out until everyone has been consulted. The professor is sensitive to cultural issues that make some people reticent to be filmed, taped, sketched, or named publicly, and she is prepared to accommodate them. Even if a few of the participants were to change their minds after the filming, modern editing could and would be used to remove them from the final production.

2c. Animal Testing

For some to suffer
For others to gain
Taints civilizations
With cruel disdain

Science seems to be slowly becoming more compassionate. As more types of animals are found to have astoundingly good memories, various types of intelligence, and emotions that humans find quite familiar, an increasing number of scientists are searching for methods to avoid animal testing without putting humans at risk. These methods include computer models or the avoidance of projects that would require the use of animals beyond stealthy observation. Most social science researchers never have to decide on whether to use animals for test subjects and never have to sacrifice other living beings as part of how they make a living. Most, but not all.

The case can be made for the importance of animal testing. *The Tao of Research* leaves that case to others. The case made herein is that research would advance, albeit most likely more slowly, if all animal testing were banned. Such a ban would be both compassionate and only temporarily restricting. As current civilizations reflect on their historical and even more their recent treatment of animals, most people consider current treatment as more enlightened. There is no evidence that the path already seen will not continue. Those who follow the path have the chance to lead it by refusing to participate in activities that include animal testing in a manner that would not be appropriate to human participants. Ask pet owners whether their pets seem to have feelings. When we think that we are sacrificing animals for our benefit, *The Tao of Research* asserts that we are sacrificing our responsibility for appropriate stewardship over all the children of this planet.

The high school principal has reflected on the matter of animal testing. He had tried for many years to find a balance that would allow both the biology department and the biology club to house live animals. He feels a responsibility to his students to foster an environment whereby they would benefit from direct exposure to the typical animals found in biology labs. Over the years, he has tried several sets of guidelines to ensure the appropriate care of the animals. Finally, he settled on "All animals will be treated as if they were beloved pets."

The director of public health is not directly involved with animal testing. Yet she is fully aware that medicine depends on the ability to conduct painful and life-shortening research on animals. Animal testing in the medical sciences has been responsible for many of the lifesaving advances commonly taken for granted in modern society. Little doubt exists that the number of human lives that have been saved is enormous. Perhaps more than in any other field of research, animal testing will likely remained "justified" through its impact on human longevity. Nonetheless, the case can be made that humans display remarkable ingenuity when faced with a difficult problem and a high degree of motivation to solve it. Human ingenuity could arguably advance medicine without the need for inhumane animal testing. The opposite case has simply not been made sufficiently.

The professor has no animal rights issues in her study, but she is often relieved to be a strict vegetarian when she is offered an exotic delicacy of animal origin. Most researchers try to be gracious guests and sample whatever is placed before them, but there is no need to violate one's own long-established dietary pattern to do so.

3. Structural (Methodological) Restrictions

Only so many ways

To get something done

Only so many conditions

To start what will come

S tructural restrictions are much like the frame of a house. Once the frame is built, the basic structure of the house is in place. Internal walls can be moved, choices made for flooring, and the like, but the basic functionality of a house is greatly restricted to only the possibilities that can be accommodated by its frame.

In much the same way, the path that a research project follows is determined by the structure upon which it is built. The constraining factors (i.e., analogous to the frame for a house) are the structural restrictions. These restrictions arise from the myriad details surrounding the genesis of the project, the interests of the researchers, and the resources and time available. In this chapter, the major overlaying categories of structural restrictions and their underlying components are discussed.

Decisions are often made based on the methodological approach to inquiry (i.e., qualitative, quantitative, or a mixture of both). Furthermore, the total resources available often largely determine the size of the participant pool. Larger participant pools result in high probabilities for statistically significant findings. Yet when participant pools become very large, functionally unimportant findings often achieve statistical significance. From the start, researchers should determine if they have the resources to achieve sufficient power for the size of the effect under study.

   a. Qualitative: thick, rich description. Inquiry tends to be open-ended and is conducted in that manner captures respondents' views as closely as possible. It is an inductive approach to knowledge generation.

   b. Quantitative: data-driven. Relies on statistical analysis (e.g., even the arithmetic mean is a statistic). Survey response categories are predetermined, rather than open-ended. Deductive approach to knowledge generation.

   c. Mixed Methods: literally, a mixture of qualitative and quantitative methods.

   d. Power: the ability to find something substantively important. Normally, the power available to research is taught as a concern, or restriction, for quantitative methods, where a sufficient sample size is needed. Yet for qualitative methods, sufficient depth, time, reasoning, and checking for information form an analogous set of concerns.

e. Data Design: to a large extent, the combination of where and how subjects (or topic materials) are available for study, in combination with the unique characteristics of the research question, determines the manner by which the research will need to be conducted.

f. Data Sources: where researchers believe they can find the fundamental information needed to answer their research questions.

The choice of a methodological approach is often driven by the types of research questions being asked. As will be shown in their individual sections, certain types of research questions lend themselves to qualitative designs, whereas others are best addressed through quantitative approaches. More frequently over time, both approaches are used in a combined format to try to achieve the best from both techniques.

Before research starts, the question of whether sufficient power exists should be raised to ensure that there are enough participants or other types of units of analysis for the purpose of the study. In short, big effects or unusual customs require fewer units of analysis than very small ones. For example, potent viruses do not need to infect many individuals before their tendency towards lethality is known. Yet the subtle or slow impact from many environmental pollutants may not be known until thousands or perhaps millions of individuals have suffered from the effects. Qualitatively, the importance of certain ceremonial garments or objects can be identified through a single observation of the manner by which they are revered. Alternatively, the relevance of a certain spice in a culture (i.e., the spice's local history, medicinal use, and culinary benefits) may take months of fieldwork, with both experts and local inhabitants, to properly understand. The point of power is to make sure that the resources are available to study the research question in sufficient depth to generate worthy knowledge. Without sufficient power, correct answers lack appropriate credibility. Simply being correct is not enough in research. In this context, we must be right enough times to make it believable.

Both the high school principal and the director of public health would prefer to conduct purely quantitative studies. Both of them have very busy day-to-day lives, and quantitative studies often can be structured to require considerably less time in the data-gathering stage of the project. Yet both of them also know that there is a need for information that is best gathered in an open-ended and interactive format, as is seen next. The sociologist is excited by the prospect of her fieldwork and considers it the heart of her personal contribution to her science. She will be quantifying responses whenever possible, but she feels that the subjective stories—the human components— are what give her research depth and texture, and above all, credibility.

3a. Qualitative

Piled higher and deeper
Left out is remiss
Thick, rich description
Is this style's true bliss

A qualitative approach is generally used when the researchers do not know enough about a situation to construct quantitative tools with predetermined response categories. Information such as age, math score, and favorite color can be categorized in advance of input from respondents. Yet issues such as the most likely event to cause a recession in the next 5 years would likely require a more open-ended approach. In that way, respondents could think of anything that mattered to them, which would be the point of gathering the information.

The actual methods used are as varied as the personalities and the creativities of the researchers. Activities such as "dashboard" sociology (i.e., literally observing from a car), open-ended questions, questions developed on the spot in response to a participant's information, personal immersion in a culture, and so on form a broad spectrum of possible approaches. Qualitative work, in short, looks to uncover more than typical numbers would tell. This type of research is often interested in answering questions that start with "Why" rather than in finding numerical relationships. These types of questions often result in complex answers involving constellations of relationships.

The result is a thick, rich description that is unabashed by results that could not be predicted in advance of conducting the research. Importantly, an inductive approach to knowledge generation is often needed. With fewer clearly recognized, understood, or previously measured pieces of information than would be normally found in quantitative work, researchers try to build a big picture from only a few of its parts. The manner by which those parts are portrayed within the big picture can form the heart of the credibility and the validity of the results. Although often characterized as more subjective than quantitative research, qualitative results have often formed the basis for later quantitative inquiries. Importantly, the argument is often made within qualitative research that credibility and validity of results arise from their logical context. Even in quantitative research, where validity is often reduced to a number, its soundness still rests on logic. Unfortunately, logic is subject to pervasive conditioning's effects, as is our other aspect of cognition—one more issue for researchers to monitor.

The high school principal will be gathering much of his data from the school's electronic student records system (i.e., quantitative). Yet he wants to create the possibility of a second line of argumentation for the project. Granted, he would prefer to have statistically sound evidence of the scholastic benefit of academic clubs, but he knows that scholastic benefits are but one of the many plausible effects from participation in a structured and supervised after-school environment. Open-ended questions (e.g., "What aspect of club membership have you enjoyed or benefited from the most?") could be used to elicit information that might be used to justify the clubs' expense, if the electronic data did not result in a statistically significant finding. Although understanding that he is not supposed to have a vested interest in the outcome of his study in order to maintain an unbiased perspective, he believes that the transparency of his process will assure any detractors that he did not predetermine the results, if in support of the clubs.

The director of public health does almost all of her work through electronic data. Even the surveys have data collected into precategorized responses. Yet investigating the extent of ordered vaccine that is not delivered does not lend itself to using portions of previously used survey items. She believes that she needs to talk to the appropriate staff at a representative sample of the clinics. These conversations will be designed to result in quantitative information for her estimations. Nonetheless, she is quite aware that she will likely be told other information that will be helpful in interpreting the results of her estimations. The political persuasiveness of this additional qualitative component should not be underestimated. A few cogently placed stakeholder quotations often can make a big difference in the credibility of an argument.

The professor wants to gather a wide array of personal views, and she is dedicating herself to learning from her study participants. Her interviews are constructed to include quantitative aspects such as demographic information and opinion surveys, but she plans to immerse herself as fully as possible in the lives of her participants. In this way, she will try to achieve a deeper understanding of each culture. The two families who will host her have promised to introduce her to many of their friends. She has been practicing both languages in preparation. The languages are very similar, so she is also hoping to learn how and why they evolved as they did. All of her participants speak at least some English, so she has little doubt that she will be able to find an interpreter in any gathering, just in case. She is hoping to improve her language and cultural skills in anticipation of future fieldwork. Research grants are highly competitive, and having strong communication skills is an asset.

3b. Quantitative

Counted or estimated
Populations are key
This method's style
Is data entry

When using numbers, the results are quantitative, or they have a quantitative component. The quantities can be of anything imaginable, but they have in common that they can be numerated, and they have importance to someone. Measurement theory comes into play. There are rules in various academic fields about how things are counted. Furthermore, there are rules about the ways in which certain types of counts can and cannot be combined. Violating these rules often leads to spurious results (i.e., the reason for the rules in the first place), as well as leading to more embarrassment than most people would prefer in their professional lives.

An enormous number of statistical methods exist. It is probably not an exaggeration to suggest that new statistics or modifications to methods are created every day, and many work through the peer-review process to become recognized methods or modifications. No single person can keep up with the emerging literature on statistical methods across all disciplines. So, as in many fields, statisticians specialize in fields ranging from sampling to theory-free multivariate analysis. Having the right type of statistician collaborate during the planning stage of a research project can be and has been critical to the validity and to the policy relevance of a project's findings.

Statisticians specialize because many rules and assumptions govern the proper use of statistics, with some more obvious than others. From determining an appropriate sample size to controlling for nonrandom characteristics, statistical advice before starting a project is usually more helpful than statistical assistance after the data have already been collected. In large measure, the advice needed is really guidance through the implicit restrictions on research from the use of quantitative statistics.

Researchers generally have more data than is needed, while also rarely having exactly the data desired. Although quantitative researchers generally use deductive reasoning to reduce the data to a cogent construct or finding, they also find that proxies must often be used. For example, although a given household's income might not be known, the median household income for the census tract is probably available. Although household incomes vary within census tract, extreme deviations are removed and overall levels of income are accommodated. For some projects, census tract information might be sufficiently valid; for other projects, it might not be accurate enough.

Critically, a major restriction from the use of quantitative statistics is due to the nature of the data collection methodology. Plausible responses must be known in advance of the data collection. Whether these responses are for arithmetic questions or for color preference in a new car, participants are limited in how they will respond. If these conditions do not exist for an item, the odds are that the item is qualitative.

The high school principal will use his electronic school record to its fullest. Yet he knows that good practice dictates that he should extract only the data that he needs. Whenever personally identifiable data are used, there is an increased risk of a breach in security. So-called fishing expeditions are rarely conducted with personally identifiable data for this reason. Having been in the business for many years, he knows the pertinent literature and has many colleagues who have worked with similar topics in their schools. The data that he will extract will include the following fields: a unique identifier, year in school, academic club memberships, related current and previous grades in the related subjects, subject-specific achievement test scores, and eligibility for free or reduced-price meals (a proxy for income).

The director of public health also will be using quantitative methods. She knows the proportion of children who have been partially or fully immunized according to her data, but she believes that the data underrepresent the true degree of adolescent immunization. Her research question about the extent to which children are being immunized in clinics without formal reporting is quantitative, but she will be gathering anecdotal information from which to estimate vaccine delivery in a quantitative manner. From the start, she realizes the inherent lack of specificity from anecdotal information, but she is hoping for a convergence of that information so that she can apply quantitative methods.

The professor will be gathering data from nearly 100 subjects over the course of her 6-month project. She has engaged the services of a doctoral student in statistics to help her with the various quantitative aspects of data collection, storage, retrieval, and manipulation. Her questions include the following: Do you believe that your culture has better rights for women than the other culture? Do you consider your culture to be truly matrilineal or patrilineal? Why do you think your culture has maintained or lost its form of lineage? Do you believe that land ownership is critical to women's empowerment? In the professor's style of inquiry, the "Do you . . ." questions are quite often followed by a "Why" question—for the thick, rich description.

3c. Mixed Methods

Something is needed
To overcome a lack
No single method
Is a worthy attack

Mixed methods are literally mixtures of qualitative and quantitative methods. The proportions of one approach versus the other are not pre-established but are the natural outcome of the study questions, available resources, and the training and disposition of the person with ultimate authority for the research protocol. Most research functions in this manner, with people sifting and sorting themselves into working with projects that match both their topical research interests as well as their favored method of inquiry.

The process of using mixed methodologies results in two conceptually different forms of validity that must be amalgamated to be useful. The quantitative side of the research garners its validity through the rigor of its technical approach combined with (often) deductive logic. The qualitative side acquires its validity through the persuasiveness of its (often) inductive logic combined with highly specific evidence from credible sources. Both methods of bolstering validity are appropriate. Notice, though, that both approaches have logic in common, although often applied in different ways. Yet it is this logic that allows researchers to blend the two types of results into a compelling argument. Given that good research starts with good research questions, the strength of the logic used in approaching answers to those questions can be the determining factor in the success of the project. For this reason, mixed methodologies are often more persuasive to nonstatistical people than are strictly quantitative approaches. This point is well understood by researchers, for without being persuasive, their new knowledge will not be put to use.

The principal, while leaning on quantitative methods, believes that his school board might be more impressed by a series of student testimonials. This information would delineate specific examples for where, when, and how the information and the approaches to inquiry that were learned in the academic clubs proved useful on tests and for papers in the associated academic courses. Whether delivered in person (the principal's preferred approach) or transcribed for documentation, these types of personal testimonials have proved themselves to be quite persuasive in most policy arenas.

The director of public health will be using qualitative information in a different manner. She needs to derive quantitative estimates for her equations for two variables. First, undocumented but vaccinated children form an unknown but potentially important segment of the population. Second, the amount of vaccine that is destroyed is also a key variable in calculating the amount that was actually delivered. Although laws are changing in some areas, her state does not require that community clinics keep records of either activity. She will need to interview the staff at several clinics, survey the rest, and compare the results. In this manner, she can see if the survey results yield the same estimates of undocumented vaccinations and destroyed vaccine as her personal interviews. Given her greater faith in personal interviews, she will use any proportionate difference in the results to adjust the estimates from the survey.

The professor is using both quantitative and qualitative approaches to her project. In addition, she is using media as a research tool. She will be showing small groups of people two ethnic films and then leading discussions about the subject matter, which includes controversial women's rights issues. Both films were very popular in west Africa within the past 10 years, so the sociologist is curious about the impact the films may have had on their cultures.

3d. Power

The size of the difference
And the size of the sample
Combine with diversity
Create an example

Power is the ability to find something substantively important. Normally, the power available to research is taught to students as a concern or restriction for quantitative methodologies. Larger samples, less variability in the information, and larger differences sought combine to increase the power of the resulting statistics. Too much power and trivially small differences will become highly statistically significant. Yet, in most cases, resource restricts function to limit the available power for all but large-scale research.

For qualitative methodologies, the analogue to power is in the consistency of independent reporting of a construct or phenomenon along with the strength of the evidence for that construct or phenomenon. Gathering this type of information without biasing the results is a difficult process that requires specialized training and often rare personality traits, such as the ability to disregard swarms of biting insects while talking with one unbothered shaman after another. But to the extent that the information gathered is essentially the same, that information's trustworthiness increases in power along analogous lines to quantitative situations. The pertinent analogies are the sample size and the variability of information gathered.

For the principal, academic clubs tend to be small but numerous. Furthermore, he has realized that many of the clubs share many of the same students. This fact presents a complicated statistical condition for which he has consulted a statistician for assistance. The principal was assured that he would have enough power to find an effect of about half of a grade point (e.g., A, B, . . .), or about five points on the typical school scale where 90 to 100 is an A. He had been hoping for better specificity than that but has resolved to put more emphasis on the personal testimonials if needed.

With the electronic medical records and population data, the director of public health has an overabundance of quantitative data. With more than 100 community clinics operating in her state, she also has ample qualitative opportunities if she can restructure her obligations to free the needed time and be granted the funding to travel to some of the more distant clinics. Overall, though, she believes that she will have more data and qualitative information available to her than she could possibly have the time or resources to use.

Our professor has access to several impeccable sources. She plans to collect copious amounts of both quantitative and qualitative data to substantiate her theories. She plans to devote a minimum of 6 months of research to this project, with minimal funding, but she needs to publish some research results to get better funding. Her techniques should produce meaningful data and insightful interviews.

3e. Data Design

The same or the many
With the when so sublime
Determine the method
Of data design

Three basic designs cover most of research: cross-sectional, longitudinal, and sequential cross-sectional. Although there are several variations of each type, final choice in data designs determines much about the statistics that can, should, and will be used in the project. A brief description of the overarching characteristics of each design is as follows:

i. Cross-sectional: a one-time, single measurement approach to the data. Group results can be compared or baseline statistics gathered, but the basic design is not meant to explore changes over time.

ii. Longitudinal: these studies have long been considered the gold standard for assessing changes over time. By using only the results from participants who were in the study for its duration, many different types of confounds are avoided. Furthermore, by comparing existing data on participants who remained in the study with data from those who did not, issues such as the generalizability of the results also can be explored.

iii. Sequential cross-sectional: when longitudinal data are either not available or are impractical to collect, repetitive cross-sectional data are often used. Similar to longitudinal data, there are at least two points in time that are measured. Dissimilar to longitudinal data, the same people are not necessarily measured each time. Although containing more ambiguity than longitudinal data, these designs are often used for public health monitoring and policy setting in a wide variety of arenas.

As was briefly explained for sequential cross-sectional data designs, the choice is not always according to which type of data would be best for the study. For example, many large-scale attempts to improve public health would be best informed by longitudinal data. Yet the necessary data tracking and collection mechanisms to follow large-scale groups are available only for relatively few national projects. Furthermore, tracking a meaningful size segment of an entire population presents enormous challenges. Even keeping track of a single family for 20 or so years can be difficult. So, nonmedical research (e.g., not pharmaceuticals, implants, etc.) and much non-life-or-death research are relegated to the less informative but still important sequential cross-sectional design.

For reasons that will become apparent in the next sections, the high school principal is planning on using a longitudinal design, and the director of public health will be using a cross-sectional design, although most of her data designs are sequential cross-sectional. The sociologist will be comparing data she collected in graduate school to her new findings, so she will be using a sequential cross-sectional design.

3e.i. Cross-Sectional

One slice in time

Criteria amassed

A momentary glimpse

Of a world now passed

Cross-sectional data answer questions about one point in time. Although they are not designed to assess change, often they can be modified to do so without much difficulty. Most often, though, cross-sectional designs are used to find out the extent of a problem, situation, or condition as a way of prioritizing improvement activities.

For these types of studies, a time period of interest is first determined. This time period needs to make conceptual sense, such as grades over a marking period in high school or flu shots delivered during an annual flu season, which crosses calendar years. When issues such as calendar, fiscal, or reporting years are crossed for the data to make sense (e.g., October in one year until March the next), the added hurdles to data collection can seem to multiply. Nonetheless, the validity of the results often hinges on the conceptual congruence of the question at hand and the time period studied.

Moreover, data must be available for at least a relevant and representative population of interest. Having data available also includes having the resources for sampling and data collection, when used. The size of the potential effort needed to collect data should not be underestimated—in number of staff, required funds, and amount of time. Furthermore, it is well known among applied researchers that real-life data carry with them unexpected problems. These problems can include differing methods of coding, collection, and storage—and that is just the start of the potential issues found in projects using all but the most scientifically controlled data.

Overall, therefore, there are three basic requirements for this type of data design. First, a conceptually relevant time period must be determined. Second, data must be within resource and other logistical reach. Third, and most important, research questions must be about a single point in time.

The director of public health has chosen a cross-sectional design because her question is about one point in time. Her estimates of the percentage of children who have been appropriately immunized have nothing to do with a change in that percentage over time. But if the result of her work is a percentage that the state's public health medical director believes is too low, she will need to revise her data design to become sequential cross-sectional. That way, she will be able to assess any change in the percentage after suitable quality improvement intervention and data stabilization periods.

3e.ii. Longitudinal

Inference restricted
But much to commend
When those at the beginning
Are there at the end

Longitudinal data have much to recommend them. The reason is that there are far too many differences in situations to experimentally control for many of them. Furthermore, these designs can be used with little actual time separating the beginning from the end. For example, studies of the effectiveness of many different types of training often give a test of the training's content before and, again, after the training. In this way, the trainers can see how much of the intended material was learned, along with where the training needs to be made more accessible. Other longitudinal studies continue for decades, such as those on heart health, cancer, and aging.

Longitudinal studies derive their exalted place in data designs from one simple fact. No human being is as similar to another as people are to themselves. Simply put, we are our own best experimental controls for many types of research situations. Certainly, concerns such as random assignment to groups are also critical to the expected rigor and to the validity of the results for many types of studies, but a longitudinal data design can often resolve many confounding issues.

Furthermore, longitudinal data can yield results that are quite different from sequential cross-sectional data, so the results can be tricky to compare because of the impact of the participants who do not remain until the end of the study. For example, when looking at academic achievement grown throughout the high school years with data from one of the largest studies of education in this country's history, the National Education Longitudinal Study (NELS), one finding was striking: the rate at which students learned (i.e., scored higher on appropriately scaled tests spanning the high school years) was lower for the longitudinal cohort and for the sequential-cross-sectional cohort (i.e., multiple cross-sectional studies of the same basic group over time).

The overarching difference between the two cohorts was that the ending 8th-grade cohort contained the students who dropped out of school before the end of the 12th grade. The 12th grade contained the more successful and longitudinal cohort of students. Yet, remarkably, the rate at which the longitudinal cohort of students gained academic knowledge was slower than the rate found for the sequential cross-sectional cohort. This effect was found across all four academic domains contained in the study. Why would a cohort that also contained less academically successful students learn faster than a cohort of high school graduates? This effect is explained in the section for sequential cross-sectional data designs, following the high school principal's reasoning for using a longitudinal data design.

The high school principal chose a longitudinal design because the natural structure of academic clubs is that students who attend more than two or three weekly meetings at the beginning of a school year normally remain in the club for the entire year. Importantly for his purpose, the ability to use pretests and posttests not only can yield quick and valuable data by themselves but can also be useful for constructing a longer term, more compelling case.

3e.iii. Sequential Cross-Sectional

Evolving social systems
Public health, rates of crime
Are sometimes best assessed
By who is there at each time

Sequential cross-sectional data designs are multiple cross-sectional designs that are applied over time to the same overall population. The influx and exiting of portions of the population are not statistically or methodologically removed from the results. This acceptance of somewhat different populations at each measurement is a hallmark of this type of data design. Yet, as briefly discussed earlier, these designs not only return different results from those seen in longitudinal designs, but they also truly answer different types of questions. The issue with the NELS data just discussed was that one question was being used for designs that are only most appropriate for different questions. Here is the way that this issue unfolded with those data.

Rate of academic achievement growth is defined as a quantifiable amount learned over a known amount of time. Both of the rates for each cohort were calculated as the difference between the average 12th-grade score and the average 8th-grade score divided by the 4 years separating the tests. Not only did the longitudinal cohort finish high school, they were the only ones finishing high school. So, the students in both the 12th-grade longitudinal cohort and in the sequential cross-section cohort were the same students. That means that the average 12th-grade score would be identical for both groups.

The 8th-grade longitudinal cohort had the more academically inclined students, and they had an average score that was higher than the other cohort, which included the dropouts. The 8th-grade average score of the sequential cross-sectional cohort was lower to start. Therefore, the change in the scores of the sequential cross-sectional cohort was larger than the change in the scores of the longitudinal cohort. The result was explainable but had not been expected—the sequential cross-sectional cohort necessarily appeared to gain in academic achievement faster than the longitudinal cohort. The reason can now be seen easily. The question presumes that it makes sense to compare the two rates of academic achievement growth, which in turn presumes that the two methodologies are comparable. This false assumption is what led to the faulty conclusion.

Our sociologist lived in west Africa during graduate school, 7 years ago, and conducted research on women's issues. Although her populations obviously differ, she has kept her original data and designed some questions to overlap and enable her to draw comparisons. Again, she will state the restrictions in her limitations section.

3f. Data Sources

Ease of attainment
Or fitness for use
The trade-offs are many
The volume profuse

For both quantitative and qualitative studies, new knowledge has to come from somewhere. If that knowledge is to gain widespread acceptance, it must be bolstered by convincing evidence. Furthermore, that knowledge and its supporting evidence should be free of plausible, rival explanations that also fit the data or information at hand.

Sources for data vary almost as much as their content. Moreover, the required arrangements for obtaining data can be as simple as a free download or as difficult as complicated procedures with lengthy registrations, security requirements, and high upfront capital costs. Furthermore, the general pattern in research seems to be that the data that best fit the research question are those that are either the most difficult or the most costly to obtain. The result is that, once more, research is a series of trade-offs. For the research to even start, one of the first tasks is to find appropriate data sources within the existing budgetary and staffing resources. Some of the most common sources of data are as follows.

Centrally Collected Databases. These types of databases generally result in far more research than is conducted by the data's parent organization. Although often used by the group that collected, coded, and stored the data, the resulting databases are very often used by others for research questions that could be addressed by those data. Regulations vary widely for researchers seeking to use these types of data, so planning considerably in advance is often required.

Governments. Governmental departments and agencies collect data (e.g., taxes, census, labor, health and human services, education) and often make those data available to qualified researchers. Every major department manages massive amounts of relevant data that, in some cases, can span decades. Often, specialized software and long learning curves are required to made profitable use of government-collected data.

Academia. The heart and soul of the scholastic pursuit of knowledge, academia generates and gathers data as part of many, if not most, graduate programs and through institutes and centers that often exist through the skillful acquisition of grant monies. These databases are often not as large or as complicated and are often more specialized than are government databases.

Private Organizations. It has often been said that information is power because of its influential capacity. When data are appropriately transformed by a compelling context, the result can be very persuasive information. Private organizations often control their data in a manner that is consistent with their business (and profit) model.

Self-Generated. Surprisingly often, no available data source has the needed data, so researchers must generate part or all of what is needed, or piece it together from various sources. The quality and objectivity of the process sets the stage for the eventual validity, and thus the worth, of the resulting information. As a general rule, when building a data set, enter the data at the most granular level possible. Data easily can be aggregated to a less granular level when needed, but data cannot be disaggregated after entry.

Surveys. Researchers often ask others to share information. Surveys can be conducted in person, by phone, by mail, by the Internet, or by any other method that could yield an interpretable context for a participant's responses.

Observation. Observation is literally watching and seeking to understand—which can also include questions for participants. So-called dashboard sociology is based on the idea that valid local information can be gained by driving around neighborhoods and carefully observing.

Electronic. Electronic archival data exist in many forms, such as tapes, floppies, and hard drives of various sizes. Before laser storage, electronic data were both written and read with magnets. Now, lasers are used to create the "0" and "1" conditions that store forms of electronic data, such as CDs and DVDs.

Hard Copy. Hard copy data are normally thought of as readable with human eyes. Yet 1960s-era, 4-bit punch-hole tape was a type of hard copy storage, as were punch cards. Nonetheless, most researchers naturally think of newspapers, paper reports, legal documents found in folders in file cabinets, and so on as hard copy data or documents.

The high school principal is planning to use both academic records and self-generated surveys, combined with personal observations and emergent questions. That one-sentence description of the principal's data sources means that the principal will be using a mixed-methods research design. The academic records are clearly quantitatively oriented; the personal observations with questions are clearly qualitatively oriented; and the survey arguably could be either, depending on its construction.

The director of public health is also employing a mixed-methods research design, as indicated by her choice of data sources. She will be using her electronic statewide database, plus she will be traveling to some of the closer clinics and telephoning others to interview personnel on the handling, recording, and disposal of vaccine. She'll be using a combination of sources for personal data gathering, in conjunction with her statewide governmental data.

The professor will be using a data set that was generated and made public by a large nongovernmental organization. She will also create her own data from her surveys and will provide rich, lifelike descriptions of her study participants that others may interpret.

4. Functional Restrictions

Reality is such

That we cannot acquire

The specificity we want

For the models we desire

Simply the way life is. The heart and soul of validity are rooted in having measures that are exactly assessing both what we think they assess and what we need for our research. To the extent that our measures are not accurate assessments, the validity of our research is compromised to some degree. Welcome to the world of applied research. The restrictions in this broad category include those related to access, the use of proxies, interpretations, results representation, measurement limitations, and error. Some of these broad categories are further granulated, such as the restrictions represented by results representation, into models, tables, and graphs.

a. Access: the ability to acquire the needed information (quantitative or qualitative) from the most valid sources, in a sufficiently timely manner for the research schedule.

b. Proxies: variables where data are available that approximate the values for the constructs we need to use in our research. For example, if we were doing large-scale research and wanted to control for (i.e., remove) the effects of income, we might need to use average income across voting districts; zip codes; or other, less granular measures than, say, household income.

c. Interpretations: bound by our own pervasive conditioning, our interpretations of data or events are colored in ways that we find hard to see and harder to avoid.

d. Results representation: pages present essentially two-dimensional information. Clever graphical and tabular representation can often display large quantities of easily accessible information, but the process of doing so is rarely intuitively obvious. Models, tables, graphs, and figures are all suspect to this form of restriction.

e. Error: in this context, four types of error are considered: sampling, measurement, estimation, and human. All four types form functional restrictions on what can be done and on the potential conclusions for the research.

f. Regression to the mean: the tendency for extreme scores (high or low) on a single measurement to change in subsequent measurements to be closer to the middle scores. Physical characteristics, such as height and weight, are not as subject to this phenomenon as are measures of educational achievement and social characteristics.

Examples of not being able to obtain the information that is really needed abound both for the high school principal and for the director of public health. For the high school principal, there is no way to figure out the unique elements taught or learned in the academic clubs to then map that information to the assessment devices in courses, while controlling for motivation, socioeconomic status, and a host of other characteristics that have long been known to be associated with both academic achievement and the rate of achievement growth.

The director of public health would rejoice at having an accurate measure for the amount of vaccine that was destroyed each year. Furthermore, she would not need that information if there were a comprehensive reporting system whereby anyone providing vaccinations had to report a certain amount of information to a central, secured source within public health. All reporting, storage, handling, and destruction of this type of data is tightly prescribed by the federal government because it has been specified as protected health information (PHI), a special class of data that must be handled in specified and secured ways. The basic tenet of PHI is this: Anything having to do with a person's medical or behavioral status that can be tied to that person is considered PHI. Beyond PHI, though, researchers have to be very careful in their handling of any information that could be considered personal and could be linked to that person through the data set.

4a. Access

Who is allowed data?

Who is restricted?

Debate continues

Researchers conflicted

Most data set owners exercise some degree of care in the release of their data because of issues regarding sensitivity and plausible release of information within a data set. Fundamentally, the more sensitive the data are, the more checks there will be on the security of the data and on the legitimacy of the researchers. For truly protected information, fines and jail sentences could await cavalier researchers. There is a spectrum that runs from data housed within a public domain site to data surrounded by extraordinary security measures with only a handful of researchers having access, so there is room for all levels and types of researchers to gain some access to others' data. Yet even researchers with stellar reputations that could span decades are often denied access to PHI and other sensitive data.

Data access does not refer only to data set access. The concept also refers to people, places, and things. For example, eyewitnesses of unimpeachable reputations are quite valuable to a very wide range of topics. The communication might be to gain background or other contextual information, or any manner of other related issue. Yet such people could now be deceased, imprisoned, too old and infirm, on the other side of the world, or state or national leaders with too busy a schedule to meet with a researcher on a particular topic. Even corporate leaders are difficult to reach for personal communication. Additionally, language issues can greatly hamper communication. Although translators are often helpful, important nuances can be lost.

Places can also function as access restrictions, and they can do so in several ways. Places can be remote, environmentally hostile, physically dangerous, or politically closed to foreigners, or they can require extreme prior conditioning just to survive. If a project included researching microbial life forms a mile below the ice in Antarctica, for example, the researchers would face an inordinately large number of physical and logistical obstacles.

Finally, things can be functional restrictions to research by being too *something,* such as too big, too small, too costly, too toxic, too rare, too dangerous, too resource intensive, and so on. People have limitations in how they can interact with the world and in the extent to which they can manipulate various tools to increase the range of that interaction (e.g., a microscope allows us to see objects too small to see otherwise). These tools that allow us to overcome these functional restrictions can also bring restrictions of their own (e.g., destructive testing).

Both the high school principal and the director of public health have full clearance for any and all data or other information collected by their respective environments. Yet both of them will have a different type of access issue—obtaining secure access for the statisticians and others who might be needed for some of the more technical aspects of the work.

The professor was denied access to the populations she most wanted to interview because she was unable to secure funding for her planned fieldwork in west Africa. She has been part of an online group concerned with women's issues in west Africa for many years and has established a substantial number of contacts in the regions of most interest to her. She also has plans to post a survey online for others to complete, but she needs to postpone that part of her project because of the limited technical resources at her college being used for her face-to-face survey results. Nonetheless, she is using innovative, local strategies that should provide valuable insights into her research question.

4b. Proxies

Not what we want
But an acceptable path
To make them more relevant
We'll get help from some math

One truism in research is that one can rarely find exactly the data that one would want to use to address the research question(s) at hand. Instead, various types of approximate data are used. By their nature, they introduce imprecision into researchers' models. The amount of error has to do with the extent to which the proxy variable captures the construct of interest. Often, median income within pre-defined geographic boundaries is used, but sometimes, there are other ways of handling it. These methods look for variables that are well correlated with the construct of interest and for which data are available.

One family of constructs that is often in need of a proxy is wealth, often assessed by personal or household income, although the value of assets (i.e., the other component to wealth) could also contribute to the models. The reason is that wealth is correlated with most events in life, from cradle to grave, from the likelihood of normal birth weight to the probability of finishing college or graduate school to overall health throughout life to age at death.

For the high school principal's project, employing the proper cross-coding and security will enable him to include whether students were eligible for free or reduced meals as a proxy for family income in his model of academic achievement growth. Doing so would yield only a crude measure of income at a point that is low on the socioeconomic scale, but it could add sufficiently to his model to be worthwhile. Because wealth and family income are correlated with academic achievement growth, as is club membership, he needs some measure to use as a control variable for this effect.

The director of public health will need to use a part qualitative and part quantitative proxy for her unobtainable information. She will be inquiring about the amount of vaccine that is typically destroyed each year and in each clinic. From her inquiries, she will estimate the distribution of destroyed vaccine across all of the clinics and other facilities where mass vaccinators dispose of unused and unreturnable serum.

The professor is using west Africans who have immigrated as proxies for those who have remained in their home countries, because all of her participants were originally from west Africa. By focusing on mostly new immigrants and including those who have come with international aid, she hopes to capture an accurate portrayal of the spectrum of opinions in both the matrilineal and patrilineal cultures. The data set from the nongovernmental organization will provide other proxies for a variety of factors (e.g., average years of schooling is a proxy for better employment).

4c. Interpretations

Pervasive conditioning

Beyond our awareness

Prevents us from accomplishing

Complete and unbridled fairness

S cience seeks to remove subjectivity from its research. Unfortunately, most social research is not ensconced within an environment that can be sufficiently manipulated along experimental lines to do that, although social researchers do try. Here is a quick example: As mentioned before, think about the manner by which scoring has changed in Olympic events. One does not have to look further than gymnastics at the summer Olympics to see that expectations on the concept of perfection have changed greatly over relatively short amounts of time. Take a judge out of time and place him or her either 20 years into the past or bring the judge from 20 years ago into current times. Both of these hypothetical judges would be unfit for service in their new Olympic games.

Researchers looking for a historical context must contend with the notion of a winner's history. Not only is the history slanted to the winner's perspective, but only that perspective is taught generation after generation. Over time, it is as though that history were the actual truth of the occurrences of the times. Under those conditions, any contrary evidence might be viewed as transcription error or something else that undermined its actual weight in the discussion.

The best that researchers can do is to be aware that their interpretations are likely to be unknowingly colored by the manner in which they have interacted with the world since birth. We are a product of our upbringing, not just in what we know and how we act but also in how we react and form judgments. As much as possible, researchers seek to limit this unwanted element by collaborating with other researchers who have quite different backgrounds but suitably complementary skills. Yet there is no way to guarantee its total removal.

Furthermore, interpretations are limited by one's own knowledge and ability to process new information in novel but informative ways. Some people are much better at seeing to the heart of an issue than are others. Similarly, some people understand political contexts better than others do, and on and on. In this manner, our own abilities limit our interpretations.

Finally, interpretations can be restrictions on our research because the findings could be used in a perverse manner to harm some individuals or groups. Researchers have to ask themselves how their information might be misused and whether their results being known are worth the risks of these same results being subverted for other reasons. Although researchers cannot have full control over the use of their published results, they do have control over how they submit those results for publication.

All three of our researcher guides know about the concept of retractions on their research because of their interpretations and knowledge, and they handle the issue somewhat differently in their research. The high school principal thinks that he can avoid most of this category of restrictions by bringing in experts in the areas where he might not have enough technical knowledge. Furthermore, he plans on interviewing several students and faculty members. Finally, he will be analyzing data for grades and for achievement gained over the year, while statistically controlling for as many extraneous factors as he can.

The director of public health is concerned about the intersection of her interpretations and the interpretations of those whom she will be interviewing. To an unquantifiable extent, each respondent will be trying to answer her through some combination of what they think to be true but in a manner that they think she will find most acceptable.

Adding to the potential confusion is the director of public health's knowledge of this situation, so she tries to understand the content through the veil of her respondents' manners of communication. The result is layers upon layers of partial communication that needs to be agglomerated through pervasively conditioned interpretations into numbers for the amount of vaccine destroyed by the clinics.

The professor has consulted with her colleagues and the college's research center, but she knows her bias is strong. She wants to believe that the female land ownership that is more commonly found in matrilineal societies is beneficial and that such cultures evolve with more equitable opportunities for women. Nonetheless, she is trying to keep her mind open to others' perceptions so she can accurately report what she hears. Distilling the weeks of data she gathers into a 10-minute video and a 30-minute presentation will require massive amounts of interpretation. She has asked a male colleague whose opinion she respects to assist her in editing her video, and she plans to test her interpretations against his as much as possible.

4d. Results Representation

Too much to discuss
Too much to show
Pick the points carefully
So others can know

*S*imilar to those times when we cannot quite find the words to express our exact intent or thoughts, so, too, our tools for representing constructs (i.e., models) and the research's results are limited. If we want to show the relationship between height and weight, we can create a scatterplot and include a "best fit" line. Think about what might need to be done to add the relationship with age on the same graph. Now add the relationship with caloric intake to the three previous variables. Perhaps the graphic needs to delineate these relationships for differing body types, too. At some point in this adding-on process, there will be too many variables for even a team of people with doctorates in graphical representations to work through a method by which all of the related data could be simultaneously presented. Yet training and ingenuity can often resolve most presentation restrictions. The key is in keeping both the research question and the written results very well constrained.

Four types of restrictions stemming from results representation are on models, tables, graphs, and figures. Each of these types of restrictions presents its own unique set of challenges in portraying research results. Interestingly, presentations that are eye-catching or intuitively appealing are often not as precise as those that line values up on graphs or present actual values, such as in tables (although some graphs also contain values within the area of the graph).

i. Models: By their nature, models are imperfect representations of reality. Furthermore, their imperfections stem from their being simplifications.

ii. Tables: Tables are excellent for portraying smaller amounts of data, especially in cross-tabular form, but tables have definite weaknesses in their abilities to portray continuous or complex relationships.

iii. Graphs: Graphs have objective frames of reference forming at least one axis, even a radial axis, which differs from figures. In this manner, graphs use an externally recognized frame of reference, often a well-known and widely accepted scale, to set the context for an interpretation of the presented information.

iv. Figures: Figures differ from graphs in that there is not necessarily even a single defined axis from which a context can be formed. For example, the growth in government spending could be shown as two dollar signs of differing size, which allows them simply to be self-referencing. Relationships between the elements in some models are also shown with figures, not graphs.

The high school principal realizes these limitations; knows his audience; and has decided to use models, graphs, and figures for the presentations of his results. The actual data will be mostly in table form and in appendices, rather than in the main portion of the written report. The board of education and other critical stakeholders historically have been moved more by emotion than by statistical reasoning. The compelling portion of his case must rest at least as much on student testimony as on graphs and figures showing increased achievement growth. The reason is that student testimony brings enthusiasm with it. This enthusiasm stirs the emotions sufficiently to overcome inertia and to implement a change in the curriculum.

The director of public health needs real values and a range of presentation methods. She is looking to overcome the weaknesses of each presentation method by strategically aligning the various methods to answer questions arising from one method by following it up with a presentation using a complementary method. In this way, she hopes to be proactive by addressing her audience's concerns before they speak them.

The professor is planning to use several types of results representation in her various reports, papers, and presentations. She is aware of the value of strong visual images and hopes that her combination of data and participant opinions will make her findings convincing.

4d.i. Models

What is crucial?
What matters not?
Include importance
And ideas are caught

Most models are figures (discussed shortly), but models have such importance to research that they are considered separately here. Models are simplifications of reality that focus on the salient aspects and disregard the less important issues. So, how does a researcher know which issues fall into which category, salient or less important? That question is at the heart of good research.

Asking and answering questions is arguably the most important pair of activities in all of research. It sets the stage for potentially generating results that might stand the test of time versus results that are soon overturned in some way. To ask and answer that question, a researcher must know the topic of interest. There is often an extensive review of the literature to learn what has been done and what is already known about the topic. The reason is that the researcher is at the starting point in a project. It is at this beginning stage that many serious confounds could be avoided through expert knowledge of a topic and methodological accommodations of the most likely of them (perhaps revisit the chapter on confounds to fully grasp the importance of this issue).

Not all researchers commit their models to paper. Yet almost all researchers maintain a mental model of the way that they believe "the system" operates with regard to their projects. Good practice, though, is to commit that model to paper. The model becomes guidance to help to focus the research, but it also forms a visual statement as to the restrictions that it imposes. Both aspects of models are important and are now considered separately.

For guidance, a model acts as a figure that shows the relationships among the various elements as well as their orientations with respect to the other elements in the model. Models can also be geographic or topographic, showing boundaries and/or overlaps between and among constructs. The point is that visual representations allow other researchers to understand the concepts and relationships in greater detail and specificity than would normally be available through vocal communication alone.

The restrictions presented by models are by way of all of the constructs and other details that are not included in the model. By definition, these not-included issues will not be addressed anywhere in the research except one very important place, the Limitations section, where plausible unaccommodated confounds are discussed. But a visual depiction of a model is the clearest explanation of those aspects that are included in the model and those that are essentially ignored.

All of our researchers have built fairly complicated models to guide and limit their projects. They will be refining their models as a start to see what is truly available for data that can be used to control for highly plausible confounds, such as the socioeconomic status of both the principal's students and the professor's west Africans, as well as the processes by which multiple-dose vaccines are destroyed.

The high school principal's model is quite simple at its center but rather complicated at the periphery. The basic concept is that course content plus related academic club participation should result in more achievement gained than just attending the course. Although the concept seems both straightforward and logically sound, it turns out to be amazingly difficult to assess accurately. The confounds are quite daunting. For a fairly long list of characteristics, students who avail themselves of academic clubs turn out to be very unlike those who do not participate. These characteristics are the confounds that often result in research that yields faulty conclusions and generates incorrect knowledge in the process. Trying to find data to accommodate these differences in a quantifiable manner comprises the fuzzy periphery currently displayed within his model.

The director of public health is really at the beginning stages of building her model. Her model resembles a flowchart. She is hoping to track related vaccine from the time it enters the state to the time it is destroyed, by quantifying each step for each facility receiving vaccine in her state. She knows that the bulk of the models will need to be estimated through samples and focused studies, but she does not see another path forward that would yield estimates of preventive coverage that are any more accurate than those previously compiled with much simpler methods.

Our professor has a geographic model with each culture's centers of population highlighted. She has superimposed the data on female land ownership and levels of education on top of the map and found the overlap strikingly informative. She is in the process of layering other parts of the data onto the geographic model to see if other persuasive patterns emerge. The sociologist has also traced the history of both cultures and modeled what she knows about their women's issues alongside the important changes in society.

4d.ii. Tables

Frequencies and cross-tabulations

The presentation is clean

Columns are lined up

Rows complete the scene

Tables can range in complexity from simple presentations with only a few cells to eye-crossing monstrosities that span several pages. Although just about no one wants to try to make sense of a several-page table, fewer than four cells with numbers in them is probably too few to justify having a table. Researchers should simply use text to present one, two, or three values.

Corresponding to the range of complexity found in different tables, the types of information and their presented relationships can greatly vary. For example, tables for means, frequencies, cross-tabulations, or correlations all present vastly different types of information.

Yet tables in general suffer from one common restriction; they are built on cells as their defining structural element. Adding multiple dimensions to show complex or continuous relationships is more difficult with tables than with graphs or figures. This construct is key to understanding the functional restriction placed upon researchers when they choose to use a table. Normally, only discrete information can be presented, such as a value or short line of text.

Nonetheless, properly designed tables are relatively quick to produce and easy to understand, and therefore, they deliver a strong impact. The trick is to have little enough to say in a table. Although there are important exceptions, tables are best for relatively small amounts of information that are central to the topic and/or the findings. All of our researchers have used at least one table in every quantitative project with which they have been associated. There is little reason to believe that trend will not continue into the present and future projects.

4d.iii. Graphs

Points, lines, bars, and colors

Good graphics create

Eye appeal and information

For the data they relate

When applicable, graphs are a comprehensible method for presenting large amounts of complex information in a small amount of space. They can have good eye appeal and be intuitively attractive, all while presenting a sufficient level of quantitative precision for the topic and the policy, program, or other question under study.

Even brief experience with computerized spreadsheets acquaints people with a wide variety of "stock" graphs—from simple bars to radial designs. When a graphical representations program is used, the variety of potential options can leave a user almost catatonic, afraid of not quite getting the right one. Sometimes, fewer choices is better, at least when what is needed is one of those choices.

The manner by which graphs are functional restrictions, though, is through the media needed and the fact that we live in three-dimensional space (neglecting a fourth dimension, time, for the present discussion). Yet counting the number of dimensions is central to the manner by which graphs present functional restrictions. Returning to an earlier example, graphing height by weight, age, and caloric intake would make most researchers pause, for a long time.

The reason is that the four variables require three spatial dimensions to graph. Here is why. When researchers want to graph three dimensions, they often use the equivalent of shadows and perspective art to give the illusion of three dimensions on the two-dimensional medium used for the presentation. Potentially, just as the shadow of a three-dimensional object is a two-dimensional object, the shadow of a four-dimensional object is a three-dimensional object. Unfortunately, humans neither think nor represent information in this way. So, we are limited in the number of dimensions to a topic that we can present in our three-dimensional world.

Granted, there are some methods of showing several dimensions on single graphs, but these types of graphs quickly start to look busy and get somewhat (or very) difficult to read. For this reason, graphs tend to deliver the most impact when they focus on two dimensions of a problem, and add a third dimension only when needed. If graphs were considered tools to deliver quick snapshots of large amounts of data, rather than overviews of the entire database, most stakeholders would gain a far better understanding of the relevant material than the small amounts gained from overstuffed, multicolored, or tiered graphs. Our guides understand the advantages as well as the functional restrictions from graphs, although all three plan on calling on specialists in graphical representations to help prepare their final reports.

4d.iv. Figures

All manner of shapes and sizes
Unbridled imagination
But not generally precision
That stands behind the creation

If it is not text, table, or graph, chances are that it is a figure, which includes illustrations. Photographs and other objects that could be embedded in a report or presentation may have their own types of restrictions, but those types of issues are beyond the scope of the present volume.

The chief restriction to figures is the difficulty in ensuring that they are not misleading. For example, if researchers wanted to show a doubling in spending through an increase in the size of dollar signs, they could double the size of the image—making it twice as high and wide. But they would have also increased the area on the page used by the image of the dollar sign by fourfold. So, they may be suggesting the idea of an increase that is actually twice as large as they had hoped to do. If they did the same thing with the representation of a pot of coins, they could unintentionally be suggesting that there was an eightfold increase, rather than the doubling that had taken place.

Figures are used only infrequently with values for coefficients or the like. Most often, they are designed for relatively low-precision situations where only the overarching constructs need to be presented. This low-precision structure engenders conversations about the bigger issues, rather than the accuracy of some decimal values or other relatively trivial issue in some larger system of policy or programmatic interactions.

Whereas all three researchers will use figures for their models, only the high school principal and the professor plan on using additional figures in their reports and in the presentations of their results. There are various aspects of the principal's work that would not benefit from the added precision of graphs but might benefit from the heightened emotional appeal that can come from figures. The professor used figures in her past research on this topic and found that she can reach a wider audience with figures than with any other form of representation. She not only hopes to present her findings to scholars and policymakers, but also plans to share her results with the study participants, some of whom have no formal education and could much more easily understand the meaning of a figure than a graph or a table.

4e. Error

Where there is signal

There will always be noise

Familiarity with the latter becomes

One of measurement's strongest ploys

Beyond simple human error, research-related error is the single largest reason that statisticians should never claim certainty. Researchers are similarly limited. Basically, if the topic is worth studying scientifically, there will be error involved in the process. Many of the most widely known advances in science and research involve new processes, equations, or constructs that greatly reduce our errors in sampling, measurement, or estimation beyond the human element.

   i. Sampling: Error in sampling comes from a lack of full representativeness. Larger samples and strategically sound methods of achieving them typically result in smaller amounts of sampling error.

  ii. Measurement: Measurement values are the sum of a true value plus the error inherent to the measurement system being used.

 iii. Estimation: There are as many types of estimation errors as there are methods of creating estimates. The point is that research results are not generally static numbers but a range of potential values from which the results are representative, but not necessarily congruent.

Much like death and taxes in life, error in research cannot be avoided. The central construct around the functional restrictions placed on researchers is in managing error in each of its forms. Most research contains several different types of errors. The trick is managing the error components so that they do not accumulate and present irresolvable confounds, which can invalidate research results.

4e.i. Sampling

Representative but not exact

That is how sampling is done

Sample size influences precision

The resource war is never fun

If researchers had unlimited funds and time, they would acquire their information from anyone and everyone who had something relevant to say on their topic. Unfortunately, the luxury to include everyone exists for only a tiny minority of researchers and topics. Everyone else is forced to employ samples and to make inferences from those samples to the universes from which the samples were derived. Even the high school principal needs to sample the academic clubs; otherwise, he would not have time to conduct the project.

The so-called gold standard of sampling is the simple random sample. In this method, all members of the population have an equal chance of being selected for the sample. When true, many good statistical outcomes can happen. Yet rarely in applied research does everyone (or every thing or event) have an equal chance of being selected for the sample.

The most fundamental concept behind sampling is the representativeness of the resulting sample. Generally speaking, larger samples prove themselves to be more representative than do smaller samples. Yet samples and sampling in general can become very complicated very quickly, especially in applied situations.

Samples can be staged, nested, stratified, proportional—all manner of not being a simple random sample. Why? Because something in the local environment made simple random sampling either impractical or in some way less efficient than some other methodology.

In short, sampling is an extraordinarily complicated field of study. The potential for different sources of error is vast, including in simple random sampling. For example, even in a relatively small community of several thousand people, there is probably no practical method for obtaining a simple random sample. Unlisted and blocked telephone numbers and cell phone regulations make telephonic methods impractical. Homelessness and illegal boarders both make door-to-door surveys unlikely to represent everyone, too. The harsh reality is that certain categories of people will be underrepresented, and others will be overrepresented. In short, for most communities, there are no accurate population counts and no way to evenly represent everyone residing there.

So, what should a researcher looking to use samples do? The answer depends on how bad it might be to reach wrong results. If no one is hurt in any way, and no one loses money or feels upset (etc.), the additional error introduced by amateurish sampling methodologies will be irrelevant. If a real problem could develop or a considerable sum of cash could be lost (etc.), engaging the services of a sampling specialist would be advisable.

The high school principal will be using all of the students in each of his selected academic clubs, but he will need to sample the clubs. To randomly sample them, all he needs to do is to list them in his spreadsheet, use the spreadsheet functions to assign a random number to each club name, sort the clubs by the values of the random numbers, and use the six clubs with the lowest numbers, which are now grouped at the top of his spreadsheet. Notice that the principal formally sorted his data so that he would not make a mistake trying to do it "by eye." He learned many years ago that interocular assessment (i.e., "looks that way to me") is a quick way to make additional mistakes, although it can lead to excellent and often testable insights with graphs and figures.

The director of public health has a stunningly complicated sample to design. All manner of vaccine-dispensing facilities from all around the state must be sampled. The sample will need to be stratified and weighted. To ensure the defensibility of her results, she has entered a line item into her budget for a sampling specialist as a consultant. The specific sampling topics where she will need assistance are the sampling methodology for drawing the sample and the sampling statistics for conducting the analyses and presenting the results.

Our professor has tried to include equivalent samples from both cultures that she is studying, but there are many more contacts from the matrilineal culture who are being proactive in inviting their friends to participate. She is reluctant to turn away new voices, so she has decided to administer formal surveys to only the first 30 people from each culture and to focus on the qualitative portion for the rest of her participants. She realizes that the manner by which she is choosing her sample (i.e., the convenience of the first 30 people in each culture) is a typical limitation to her type of work. Random sampling is simply impractical for her type of work. Her reports and productions will certainly contain this noted limitation.

4e.ii. Measurement

A ruler or a survey

A method to anoint

Yet tolerance is a virtue

But only to a point

All measurement contains error. Granted, some of the error is trivially small and can be safely ignored—but not all of it. To start thinking of measurement error, consider height and weight. Physicians measure both to a precision that is sufficient for their monitoring purposes. Yet their measurements are quite crude by scientific standards. Weight is usually no more accurate than to the half-pound and usually to the pound. Scientifically, plus or minus that amount of error can make a very large difference in some situations. Height is rarely assessed more accurately than the quarter inch. Again, a quarter of an inch can be a very long distance and a large amount of error in some situations.

Similar to height and weight, whatever one measures will be the sum of a true value plus an error component of a size that is intrinsically dictated by the measurement system being used. This point is important to understand. The key to measurement is to use a system whereby the inherent error is functionally noncontributory to the purpose of the measurement. For height and weight in a physician's offices, the inherent error is simply unimportant to the longitudinal tracking being done by the office.

Mental traits and attributes are arguably more difficult to measure than are physical traits. The reason is that researchers cannot physically measure such mental traits but must infer them from other types of measurements. For example, researchers cannot measure a part of the brain to find out exactly how much and the types and extent of mathematics that someone might know. They infer that knowledge from carefully designed, piloted, and validated tests, when they do it correctly. Other times, people (e.g., teachers) simply make up a test based on their own personal knowledge of a topic and hope that its face validity (i.e., looks appropriate to an expert in the field) is sufficient to give it acceptable credibility as an impartial and accurate grading tool.

The high school principal is using course grades as his measure of academic achievement. Yet he has an interesting complication to his grades. He has four types of grading systems that teachers use at his school: scores on tests that accompany the textbooks, scores on teacher-made tests, the first method plus essays, the second method plus essays. The principal is in ongoing discussions with the district's consulting statistician to figure out if he can tease out the different effects of the grade systems or if he will just have to ignore the differences and add the issue to his Limitations section in his report. He would like to know if there are differences in the resulting grades due to the systems themselves, but that concept likely will have to be tested in a separate project.

The director of public health's entire project is about reducing the proportion of error in her measurements when determining the extent of available vaccine that has been actually administered to the population. Furthermore, the extent that vaccines requiring multiple doses are actually administered, as opposed to having additional people who are underimmunized with the same amount of used vaccine, is also a large unknown for her population. Estimating health care coverage for almost any topic is difficult at the population level, but vaccinations present special challenges. Again, she will be relying on the advice of her department's statistician and research methodologist for assistance in untangling and formally estimating some of the pieces that previously have been close to pure guesses.

The professor hopes to minimize the error in her measurements by conducting all of the surveys herself. At the research methodologist's suggestion, she also plans to input all of the data herself so that she can immerse herself in the information and tease the subtle nuances from its depths. One thing she knows is that data transformed by a context become information. She already knows that many of the women in the matrilineal culture think they have more equal rights than their counterparts in the patrilineal culture, but she suspects that the older generations have a different outlook from the younger ones. She has not had any real conversations with the men from either group and suspects there is also a generational aspect to their opinions.

4e.iii. Estimation

Close enough?

How is that known?

Quantify the amount

Uncertainty should be shown

Beyond sampling and measurement error, there is the error of estimation. All methods of estimation contain error, and some methods are specifically designed to highlight the error component. For example, positive predictive validity is a technique that returns the percentage of cases with a condition among those who were predicted to have it. In health care, sensitivity is defined as the percentage of cases who have a given condition who are identified as having the condition by whatever testing is used.

Listing and defining potentially dozens of types of estimation error and methods that highlight estimation error is well beyond the scope of this book. The point of the issue is to be aware that a single value returned by a computer is generally the center of a range of potential values that could be the correct result. This issue is the reason for confidence intervals that return a range of values instead of a single point estimate.

The best way to limit error of estimation is to limit all the sources of error over which researchers have some degree of control. Even doing so, however, does not mitigate the error inherent to some estimation methods, such as multiple regression analysis, where several contributory variables are assessed for their unique contribution to explaining variability in a variable of interest. For example, students' eventual income could be the target variable of interest. Contributory variables could be years of education, parents' socioeconomic status, prestige of schools attended, and so on.

The high school principal will, in fact, be using multiple regression analysis. His model of student achievement and achievement growth requires that he be able to adjust for salient student characteristics due to academic club members not being fully representative of nonacademic club members. As an example, very few of the academic club members have part-time jobs, whereas a fairly large proportion of the students who are not in the clubs maintain a part-time job.

As has likely become self-evident, the director of public health's project centers on limiting errors associated with estimations of vaccine usage and destruction at many levels and throughout her state. To accomplish her task of a better estimate than the largely guess-based estimates of the past, she needs to concentrate on each aspect of her project to explore local error reduction methodologies wherever possible. She has no delusions about being able to return fully accurate results. Her goal is improvement, which is all that would be practical under her circumstances.

Our professor's mixed methods will show two sides of the issue. Quantitatively, her error of estimation will be somewhat small, as her models are not statistically complex. Qualitatively, her error of estimation is really an interpretive issue, both from the participants' perspectives and from hers. Participants are trying to say things in a way that they think will be more acceptable to her, compared with if they had said the same things in a different way—or in a different physical situation. Sorting through these types of nuances in our language, due to how we interact with others, is her qualitative equivalent of estimation error.

4f. Regression to the Mean

Found extreme only once
Why is no riddle
Using multiple measures
Scores move to the middle

Recall that measurements are the sum of the truth plus error. In this context, error has some special attributes that statisticians capitalize on when seeking estimates that are as close to the truth as possible. A key attribute is that, over time, errors will cancel or sum to zero because errors form a normal distribution that is randomly distributed around a mean value of zero and are assumed to be independent of each other. Yet, in the process of summing to zero over multiple measurements, errors can have a substantial impact on observed scores or measurements. When this process starts, the measurements that were farthest from the average of the measurements most likely have large error components, in addition to their true scores. Upon subsequent measurement, these randomly distributed error components likely will be closer to the mean or even on the other side of the mean, compared with the first measurement. When the measurements are taken as a group, the first score is seen to move toward the mean with the addition of the subsequent scores. This process is known as regression to the mean.

Functionally, regression to the mean dictates that it is methodologically inappropriate to use the rank orderings from a single set of measurements to determine high-stakes issues. The reason is that the cases at both the top and the bottom are unlikely to represent the true extremes from the tested cases. Only after multiple measurements should such a ranking be formed.

The high school principal knows all about regression to the mean. Every year, his school administers placement tests. Every year, he has to re-place students who were placed incorrectly into the top and the bottom classes because of large error components in their placement test scores. He would much rather use a battery of test results, but doing so is prohibitively expensive and requires too much time from students that could be devoted to instructional activities. To limit the impact of regression to the mean in his present study, the principal would likely limit his sample of clubs to those that require a year in the subject before entry into the club—such as Conversational French. But his high school does not have a sufficient number of such academic clubs for this restriction to be functionally reasonable. The result is that he will need to use early course grades compared with end-of-course grades. The end-of-course grades are better estimates, having had a larger number of multiple measurements than would have the early course grades. Given this situation, the principal has already started the Limitations section of his final report. Contemporaneously adding to a Limitations section helps to ensure its completeness.

The director of public health is not rank ordering or scoring in her project. For her, regression to the mean will become important when pay-for-performance in health care truly takes root in her state (i.e., when physicians are paid more when they follow specific treatment guidelines more closely, such as flu shots for eligible elderly). For now, her project involves a single estimate that is not designed to determine best or worst, highest or lowest of anything.

The professor has considered how to implement multiple surveys within the time constraints of her project. She has data from 7 years ago, but her topic was not precisely the same, so the number of comparisons using the two data sets will be limited. Because she will be staying with the families for a week, and they will be viewing two movies that make strong social statements, she plans to administer the same opinion survey to the household residents at the beginning and end of her stay. It seems likely that some opinions will change after a week of discussion and introspection. Although it would be better if she could wave a magic wand over their heads so that they did not remember their original responses during the second administration of her survey, a week's separation between administrations is the best that she can do.

5. Technical Restrictions

Reducing to practice

Technicalities abound

Pay heed in advance

And information is found

Technical restrictions are imposed on researchers because of the nature of the tools that they use. If a carpenter had only a hammer, it would be difficult to cut wood smoothly to a given length. So, too, the tools available to researchers both enable them as well as restrict them. The central element to understanding technical restrictions is to learn to keep results, discussions, and conclusions contained to what is allowed within the restrictions stemming from the tools. Eight categories of technical restrictions are discussed here.

a. Sample size: Although the topic is best left to statisticians, larger samples are generally better than smaller ones, yet available resources usually place limits that researchers must accept.

b. Level of measurement: Measurements have different characteristics and, accordingly, are suitable for use with different statistical techniques.

c. Descriptions versus inferences: Descriptions are about the cases that were studied, where as inferences are made to the parent populations of samples that were studied.

d. Central tendencies: Typical values are central tendencies. Nonetheless, the estimation of the typical values differs along several lines, depending upon the level of measurement of the data and, notably, the intent of the author.

e. Inequality: Inequality is information content for quantitative systems. The greater the inequality, the greater the amount of quantitative information content. Were all cases to yield identical measurements, the values would be worthless for most quantitative purposes. Quantitative research depends upon inequality. The natural extension of that concept is that research yields new information; therefore, new information generation depends upon the existence of inequality. Get comfortable with it—just never in situations where discrimination is involved (race, gender, age, etc.). Qualitative research places more value on measures that could yield the same results for entire populations.

f. Association: Relationships are associations. Associations do not imply and certainly do not confer causality. Yet associations are patterns that are better described and are more predictable than randomness.

g. Randomness: Randomness is unpredictability, no underlying order.

h. Complexity: Nesting and manifest versus latent traits are the two types of complexity discussed herein. Be aware, however, that many other types of complexity exist. When in doubt, the appropriate experts are generally available and typically charge no more per hour than many professionals whom business and private individuals often employ.

Technical restrictions are often the most daunting of all of the categories discussed herein, because there is little that a researcher can do most times to lessen the impact of each type of restriction within the category of technical restrictions. Consider them to be part of life when conducting research. Our guides understand this harsh reality of research. Nonetheless, this category of restrictions is also the class of technical concerns that brings credibility, validity, and acceptability to carefully considered and constrained research results.

5a. Sample Size

Too many is wasteful

Too few can be worse

Balance the need for precision

Against the size of the purse

S ampling is a statistical response to limited resources. It is an efficient method for estimating values (i.e., making educated guesses) for large groups. Several families of sampling techniques exist, with each type designed to handle specific types of conditions. The starting point to estimating sample size, though, is to answer the question: How big (or small) of a difference do you want (or need) to find? For example, how large a sample might be needed to see whether a professional football player could break a glass bottle with a baseball bat? One. How large a sample might be needed to see the extent to which thinking "light" thoughts could result in weight loss? A lot more than one. Big things are easier to find. Small things are harder. The rest of sampling is a continuation of that simple statement. The harder part of sampling is calculating the smallest size difference that is substantively important for the topic at hand and then seeing whether resources will permit sampling to the resultant number of needed cases.

Determining the specifics behind a choice in sampling methods and the required sample size are topics that are well left to statisticians, who often debate the topic among themselves. Much of the process is driven by equations, but the process also is driven by judgmental accommodations of the unique conditions existing at the time. Moving quickly from the tidy examples in sampling textbooks to the world of applied research, many of the conditions and assumptions in the texts are absent or contradictory in the field—greatly complicating the issue of a required sample size.

The result for most people is that just about any sampling method-ology beyond a random sample should probably involve a sampling specialist to determine sample size, as well as sampling method-ology. The methodology becomes complicated quickly, and the statistics have to disentangle the intentional nonrandomness of the methodology before being substantively interpretable.

As has already been established, all three of our researchers will accommodate the technical restrictions imposed by sample size through the use of sampling specialists. They understand that the credibility of both their results and their own reputations could be at stake.

5b. Level of Measurement

To make sense of the data
And the analysis, too
The techniques that are appropriate
Are restricted, it is true

The foundation for choosing among potential statistical techniques is the level of measurement of the data. Some statistics are appropriate for certain levels of measurement but not for other levels. This area is one where a deeper understanding of the structure of the data is needed in order to know which statistics would be meaningful. For example, the data's level of measurement limits the choice of the most often-used statistic—the average. There are three common choices of averages: the mean, median, and mode (with somewhat esoteric versions within each). These different types of averages are not equally appropriate for data at different levels of measurement. Arithmetic averages are what is typically meant by average. Yet this type of average does not make sense for some things, such as color preference or religiosity. Fortunately, many statistical techniques have options that can account for at least two of the four basic levels of measurement.

   i. Nominal: Measures are distinct, but not really larger or smaller.

  ii. Ordinal: Measures can be said to be larger or smaller (or more or less) than other measures, but the distances between the values are not necessarily equal.

   iii. Interval: Equal distances between measures on a scale, but no true zero.

   iv. Ratio: Equal distances on a scale plus a true zero.

Important to generating correct results are the recognition and accommodation of each variable's level of measurement. Even researchers with decades of experience occasionally will be embarrassed by having used a statistic in a way that was inconsistent with the level of measurement requirements of that statistic. For this reason, our researchers will have the assistance of their local statisticians at each critical stage of their projects, including the written reports and presentations.

5b.i. Nominal

Differences are recognized
Yet "more" or "less" do not apply
Category counts can be formed
Often charted with a pie

The nominal level of measurement is about categories. Some statisticians refer to this level of measurement as categorical. The members across categories have characteristics that differ but are not quantified as to the amount of that difference. For example, political party, religious affiliation, gender, and so forth can be recorded, grouped, and counted. Yet we do not say that one religion is more of a religion than another.

Under certain conditions, the most typical type of average, the mean (i.e., arithmetic average), is appropriate for nominal data. The most common of those conditions is where a variable has only two possible responses, and talking about the percentage that corresponds to one of those responses makes sense. With gender coded "0" for female and "1" for male, it would make sense to use the mean to say that a group is 60% male.

Variables coded and interpreted as we have just seen find use in a variety of statistical techniques requiring at least interval levels of measurement (a discussion about interval-level data is coming shortly). Some nominal data, therefore, can be quite useful in answering a surprisingly broad range of questions.

All of the researchers have nominal data. The high school principal has data on gender, school club membership, sports participation, and scholastic topics for each student. Some aspects of these measures could be coded as nominal, such as variables for the names of extra-curricular activities (e.g., yearbook).

The director of public health has access to a host of demographic data that are nominal, such as ethnicity and zip code. Generally, nominal data are summarized in tables or cross-tabulations of two characteristics, such as sports participation by gender or immunization rates by age or age grouping. Nominal data also delineate many of the groups of interest to research.

The professor will be collecting demographic data (e.g., gender) and asking yes/no questions that can be coded as nominal.

5b.ii. Ordinal

"More" or "less" seems to fit
But the scale is not linear
Some steps are wide
Whereas others are skinnier

Ordinal measurement is common for opinion polls. We can distinguish between levels of agreement but cannot be sure that the psychological distance between pairs of adjoining response choices are equivalent. For example, the psychological distance between "strongly disagree" and "moderately disagree" might not be the same as the distance between "neutral" and "moderately agree." In these cases, an arithmetic average (the mean) might not yield an interpretable answer.

The high school principal has ordinal scales from some student surveys that he has already conducted and of which he might generate more. Although the case could be made that course grades are really ordinal, they have been and continue to be used as interval (the next topic) since their creation. The debate is whether the difference in knowledge of a topic between two students scoring, say, 20 and 60 points on a test is the same as that between two students scoring 60 and 100 points—both pairs of students separated in "knowledge" by 40 points.

Along with actual medical data, the director of public health has results for perception surveys on the services received by the state's medical assistance recipients, including vaccinations. She also has another survey to be implemented fairly soon, a state requirement of her department. Most of her medical data, however, are either nominal or ratio, at least in how they are handled.

The professor plans to gather a considerable amount of ordinal data during her surveys (e.g., intensity of perceptions on women's rights) and has consulted with her college's research center on how best to code and process the data she collects.

For statistics appropriate to ordinal data, the three researchers will use frequency counts for the responses to each of their survey's items. All of them will use medians and modes (discussed later) to describe the affected central tendencies in their reports and presentations.

5b.iii. Interval

Nice even steps
Could walk with closed eyes
From data of this sort
Many statistics can advise

Interval data have evenly spaced steps but no true zero. Course grades could be an example, where a zero score on a math test does not mean a complete lack of mathematics knowledge. A zero on a math test means that the student did not arrive at a single correct answer for the sample of possibly relevant mathematics questions on the test. Yet the test has no way of capturing whether the student has any knowledge of the assessed topic. The zero is a measurement convenience.

Many statistics require interval levels of measurement (or ratio level, discussed next) to yield valid results. Topics from grading differences in sections of the same course to the predicted flu infection rates for next year generally require this level of data. At a minimum, some reflection on the part of researchers is appropriate when determining which statistics will be used with the data.

Examples of true interval data are somewhat rare. The most common are Fahrenheit and Celsius scales to measure temperature. Overall, the interval level of measurement is important to the proper selection, use, and interpretation of statistical methods, but it has few true examples in daily practice.

For the high school principal, most student achievement measurements are used as though they were at an interval level of measurement.

The continuing debate over the appropriateness of this almost imposed level of measurement for student grades, over a century since its inception, is testimony to the resiliency of the arithmetic mean to reasonably minor violations of its required level of measurement.

As mentioned, much of the director of public health's data are nominal but with only two possible responses. For example, immunizations are coded for people in one of two ways, either yes (1) or no (0). These types of data generally can be used in statistical techniques that assume interval levels of measurement, such as arithmetic means and multiple regression analysis.

The professor has interval data insofar as some of her data are dichotomously coded (e.g., yes/no, male/female), and these types of really nominal data can be used as though they were interval.

5b.iv. Ratio

The pinnacle of data
Most flexible to use
A true zero and even steps
Are two valuable clues

A ratio level of measurement scale has a true zero and is the trophy of data types. Weight and height are examples. We can say that half of 100 pounds is 50 pounds, and twice 6 feet is 12 feet. In other words, we can form interpretable ratios. These types of data are almost carefree in their use with regard to their level of measurement. The reason is that the vast majority of esoteric modifications of statistics (e.g., many of the options for methods in statistical software packages) were developed to account for either the lack of ratio data or sampling conditions that were neither simple nor random.

The high school maintains basic health information in the nurse's office on such things as height, weight, and inoculations, but the high school principal would likely need a good reason to be granted access to much of these data. The principal does have, however, somewhat unlimited access to absentee and tardiness information. These variables are at a ratio level of measurement. Depending on how the data are coded and used, they could be at any of the levels of measurement. Recoding (assigning new codes after the fact) can further complicate an understanding of the data's true level of measurement.

The director of public health has electronic medical information for all Medicaid recipients in her state, although restrictions on the data's use are quite stringent. Nonetheless, for a variety of purposes, she might have access to any of the types of information, including measures that have true zeros. For example, when looking at the degree of compliance with national pediatric immunization guidelines, she knows the number of different immunizations appropriate to children and the number of immunizations that should be delivered. Knowing who received which immunizations and counting them for each child, she can form ratio scales for immunization counts and for rates of immunization compliance. The more of her data that are measured on interval and ratio scales, the larger the variety of statistical techniques that will be available. As we have seen, though, gathering the basic data for this process is going to be very complicated.

Our professor also has an interest in the relationship between matrilineal cultures and nutrition. She intends to gather dietary information along with approximate height and weight. If her hunch is correct, she should see healthier body mass indexes, less chronic disease, and other differences that she might not think about in advance of her current study. The height and weight information, for example, is at a ratio level of measurement.

5c. Descriptions Versus Inferences

Talk about who is there
Or the group they are from
Describe or infer
They are not the same one

The two basic branches of statistics, in particular, and of research, in general, are descriptive and inferential. Descriptive statistics and research discuss the data at hand. No projections are made to larger or other groups. Meaningful comparisons are not made because doing so directly would not accommodate sampling error.

Nonetheless, a fundamental goal of research is to be able to project findings to larger groups or to compare groups. When inferences are made about overall populations from the findings in samples, or a comparison of group characteristics is needed, researchers are using inferential statistics. As they do this, they accommodate sampling error and generate educated guesses by way of mathematical formulas and the like.

Simply put, descriptive statistics describe data, and inferential statistics make inferences from the data to parent or to substantively similar situations or conditions. Most research uses both types, descriptive and inferential. First, descriptive statistics are used to present the salient characteristics of the data so that audiences can have the needed background to make informed decisions about the results. The population is described as best as is possible. Then the sample is described such that a reasonable person would probably think that it well represents the population. When certain aspects show a larger difference than others do, normally there will be text that recognizes and downplays the difference. Next, in the more technical statistical portion, inferential statistics are used to place the research in a larger and more important context than just the specifics of the project at hand. This section of a report is critical for publication in many top journals and can influence one's chances at continued or additional independent funding.

Most researchers refer to central tendencies and grouped frequencies as descriptive statistics. Means, medians, modes, sums, ranges, percentage cutpoints, and percentiles are all types of descriptive statistics, plus there are many more. Importantly, each of these statistics describes a different aspect of the data.

Most inferential statistics involve statistical tests. Questions about, say, whether a rate of flu immunization for the state was above a targeted goal or was higher than that of a neighboring state are types of inferential questions. When you see a statement about something being statistically significant (or not), inferential statistics were almost assuredly used.

The high school principal has questions of an inferential nature because he will have samples. He has no choice, due to the length of time it takes to get some of the data into the electronic form he needs for his evaluation. He will be using descriptive statistics in discussing the makeup of his school, the academic clubs, and the clubs specifically in his sample in his report and in his presentations to parents and the school board.

The director of public health has a more fluid population but still uses both descriptive and inferential statistics. She still believes that there is inherent sampling error in all of her data but describes her data as snapshots in time in several of her reports. Because of the large numbers of people available to her through electronic records, she believes that her data are mostly representative of everyone coming into and leaving the state's system.

In public health, almost all of the director's work involves making inferences about the effects of public policies on people's lives. Even when she groups people by age ranges, she lists likely error ranges for her statistics. She has seen where people have remembered trivially sized differences as one group doing better than another, and these same people were then surprised to see the relationships reversed in another report. By showing these error ranges (i.e., confidence intervals) from an inferential perspective, she protects the integrity of her department's work.

The professor will also be using mostly descriptive statistics. Although she is using a mixed methodology, her quantitative work is composed of simple ratios and averages (i.e., means). Her inferential results will be qualitative and relate to conditions in west Africa. Her goal is to secure more funding for future fieldwork, and she needs the descriptive data to support her inferential findings. Her access to a new descriptive data set that addresses the issues she studies is vitally important to her project; however, her field experience will fill in the gaps that the numbers cannot explain. In addition, she has a secondary goal of writing a book based on her personal experiences with both cultures. She kept a private journal 7 years ago while in west Africa, and she began an updated version recently, soon after she met with the first of her study participants.

5d. Central Tendencies

The use of an "average"
Can be naïve or well planned
Knowledge of the difference
Is worthwhile to command

M any people first dislike research methodology or statistics when introduced to central tendencies. No surprise. The topic begins by making something complicated that should be simple: an average. First, it gets a special name—central tendency— and presents three very different choices (mean, median, and mode, covered next). Many students are then required to calculate several of each, as though struggling for a few hours makes them feel better about it.

The choice of central tendency is largely determined by the structure of the data—mostly level of measurement and, to some degree, skewness. Here, researchers often find themselves in one of four positions:

(1) They know what they are doing and choose the correct average for their data.

(2) They think they know what they are doing, meaning that their choice is somewhat left to chance.

(3) They know that they do not know enough to be sure that they are making the right choice, so they get some help.

(4) They do not have a clue that they are doing something wrong.

Yes, there are other combinations, such as those who know that they are less than optimally informed but go ahead and pick a method anyway. Yet most people conducting research care about the integrity and interpretability of their results and do not want to mislead others or embarrass themselves.

i. Mean: the arithmetic average—the statistic that most people are referring to when they say 'average'—a type of weighted middle ground.

ii. Median: the value where half the data points are above it and half the data points are below it—how far above or below is irrelevant.

iii. Mode: the most common value in a dataset, regardless of where it falls.

Strategic points for statistical help in research projects include, at least, the conception of the project, during preparation of the data for statistical use, for special cases where one really should have a statistician running the statistics, and for precise nuances in interpreting the results. Although all our research guides have been known to be a bit expedient when doing their research to save time and expenses, they have done so with the knowledge that they were more likely to have to recall their results than when they involve more experienced statistical and research help. When the stakes are high, they all know to seek professional assistance.

5d.i. Mean

All numbers count
For the values they are
All summed then divided
Be they close or be they far

The mean is an arithmetic average; it has intuitive appeal, and it is the most common incarnation of the average or central tendency. Yet it needs a fairly symmetric distribution (such as the normal curve) to be a relevant approximation of the central tendency. Large outliers (e.g., a few huge salaries) can greatly distort the mean as a measure of central tendency. When the data are fairly symmetrical, the mean is quite useful. It contains more information than the median or the mode because it is affected by both the number and the size of all occurrences. Means are also quite handy for variables that only take two values, such as gender. As seen earlier, if the two values are coded 0 and 1, the mean is the percentage of the total that is coded as 1.

Nonetheless, the mean can be a difficult concept. Let us say that a group is 60% male. What does it mean to say that the average person in the group is 60% male? When one foot is in scalding water and the other in ice water, how consoling is it that, on average, the temperature is fairly comfortable? Think about the interpretations of the mean before just using it.

The high school principal will be using means for scholastic data. He has already used these data to see whether grading differences existed across his various teachers of the same subject. Then, he compared the mean grades for different sections of the same courses for similarly academically inclined students. Where large differences were found, he spoke with the teachers about resolving them, which they did through employing a common final exam.

The director of public health uses means extensively. For example, she looks for the average (i.e., mean) number of immunizations as well as various kinds of important medical services. Where large mean differences are found, she looks for associated conditions that might be actionable by policy.

The professor also uses means throughout her research. She is hoping to be able to say that a certain percentage of west Africans believe that matrilineal cultures have more equal rights for women than patrilineal cultures. She then plans to support that particular cultural belief with data from the nongovernmental organization's report. She will be comparing cross-tabulated results for each segment of her population and reporting the most interesting findings.

5d.ii. Median

Halfway through the list
The middle is a pleasure
The average of choice
For an ordinal measure

Medians are rarely used by choice. They are simply the point where half the values are larger and half are smaller. Needing only an ordinal level of measurement, they are a good choice for perception scales.

The 50th percentile is the point where 50% of the scores are below it and 50% are above it—the median. Often, the 5th, 10th, 25th, 50th, 75th, 90th, and 95th percentiles (known as cutpoints) are shown as a way to characterize an ordinal distribution. Surprisingly, interval and ratio data also are characterized this way in many settings, even though other statistics exist to describe such data. This appeal is known to conference presenters along with journal authors, as they often use this distribution. The reason is that percentile cutpoints simply have intuitive appeal. Notice that, when discussing means, percentages were employed, but when the topic turned to medians, percentiles became the units of measure. The reason is that medians are used for ordinal data, which is consistent with using medians and percentiles, whereas interval and ratio data can form true means and percentages.

If a researcher had to live with only one form of central tendency, a good argument could be made for that choice being the median. In a symmetric (balanced) distribution, the mean and the median are the same value. To the extent that they differ in value, the median becomes more meaningful and the mean less so for many situations. Why? The reason is that the less symmetrical a distribution, the more the mean represents the impact of a few larger and larger outliers.

The median is, therefore, the more stable of the two forms of central tendency discussed so far. It does not require a symmetric distribution, so it functions well with either type of data.

All of our researchers will be using the median for data gained from percentile scales. Many of the high school principal's standardized test scores are best displayed as percentiles. The director of public health also will use percentiles to explain the distributions of immunizations and other services for various groups in her state in her final report. The professor has participants who fall into a wide range of socioeconomic categories, from impoverished refugees to college professors; so, percentiles are much more descriptive of the true nature of her participant pool.

5d.iii. Mode

More of this type
Than any other choice
The highest count
Gives the mode its voice

The mode is the value with the most frequent occurrence. For data that take a large number of very specific values (e.g., length of each road in a state), the mode is not useful. For data that take a more limited number of values (e.g., make and model of registered vehicles), the mode can be informative and useful (e.g., America's 10 most popular cars). The majority of distributions can be accommodated using modes, yet it is the least informative of averages, the central tendencies. That relative lack of information content is due to the mode's failure to indicate its relationship to points anywhere else in the distribution.

Moreover, stakeholders have to guess at the mode's relative contribution to the entire distribution. For example, one would expect the mode to be zero for the number of automobile accidents a typical driver might have in a 1-year period, or it could be 12 for the number of eggs in a dozen that survive the trip home from the store. Yet many of us have never seen the mode used, although its meaning is straightforward and its potential uses are many, especially in commerce.

Both the high school principal and the director of public health will be using the mode as little as possible and hope to avoid it altogether. It is simply the central tendency of last resort. The reason is that it is the average that carries the least amount of information and is also most contingent on artifacts of scaling and methodology. The professor has used the mode successfully in scholarly presentations and plans to do so again because of the highly skewed nature of her participants' information. The mode can be useful for devising attractive graphs and figures.

The high school principal remembers an energetic discussion with a parents' group when he tried using the mode to describe the average grade at his school. The director of public health remembers the governor's speechwriter calling at midnight to get her to replace a section of a talk, which the governor was to present the next day, that involved the use of the mode. Both people are now reluctant to ever use the mode again.

5e. Inequality

Information content

Found in data's spread

Rather than studying just the middle

All measurements should be read

Differences are important. Differences are information. Furthermore, knowing *why* something or someone is different is generally more important and of more practical value than knowing *how* they are different. Admittedly, however, knowing how people or events are different forms the basis for the art of choosing the right statistical technique. Two types of inequalities are considered here—frequency distributions and standard deviations.

   i. Frequency distributions: Frequency distribution can be both text (i.e., written values) and graphics (e.g., box and whisker) based and presented.

  ii. Standard deviation: The standard deviation is a measure of dispersion around a central tendency, such as a mean.

Understanding inequality is at the core of understanding the concept of an outlier. The further a measurement is from the central tendency of the measures, the more it seems as though it might be a mistake—be it a transcription error or other type. The central tenet of outlier analysis is to determine which measurements are likely to be reflective of the truth (and keep these) versus which are quite unlikely to represent reality (reject these).

For example, if a researcher were using age in an equation, some-one with an age of 97 probably would be considered to have a legitimate age. Yet an age of 137 would be more than suspect; it would be rejected as a mistake.

All statistical analyses, and research in general, depend upon inequalities to return legitimate values. No inequality means no information, which means no results. Although it might offend some people's democratic sensibilities, inequalities are the heart, soul, and motivation behind the vast majority of social research.

All three of our professionals understand the research potential of inequality without the emotional attachment to the word so often found in typical speech. They understand that comprehending and quantifying the inequalities in their respective projects is at the core of instigating meaningful change in their respective systems of operation.

5e.i. Frequency Distributions

All levels of measurement

Can be portrayed in this way

Scores and their placements

None go astray

Frequencies are counts. What they count and how the counts are split into groups mainly depend on the research question, but fre-quently they also depend to some extent on the data (i.e., their levels of measurement and distributions). Frequency distributions are meant to convey a sense of both absolute and comparative magnitudes. Both counts and percentages are generally used to present this information. Usually, researchers do not see more than about six or eight groups, except when they fall naturally into other categories, such as the 50 states (plus Washington, D.C.). Even then, the categories often are regrouped into a smaller number of categories (e.g., New England, Midwest).

To address the questions of who, what, where, when, why, and how, researchers need to know the manner by which the data are spread and shaped. The normal, bell-shaped curve is arguably the most common and, therefore, important shape (i.e., distribution) in research. Knowing about distributions is part of matching the correct technique with the question. Further complicating the issue of distributions is that statistics have their own distributions. The term sounds deceptively simple for what it really entails. Fortunately, many statistics that rely on the normal curve are sufficiently robust to even moderately large violations of their assumptions that the results can be fairly close to what would be found if the distributions were closer to so-called normal.

Distributions are sources of information about the inequality of characteristics. Knowing about inequalities is the first step in overcoming them. Research results presented in a context become a tool of policy and a lever for a perspective. Think of this point often. When researching inequality, one often is seen as passing judgment on policy and practice. That result is because policy and practice normally claim to be focused on reducing inequalities. So, reporting inequalities could be interpreted as the relevant policy being a failure because there is still a need for it. In fact, the opposite could be true. The policy could be filling a need so successfully that more of those with that need are being served by the policy all the time, such as pre-reform welfare used to encourage dependency by making it more attractive for many types of people to stay on welfare, rather than to find work.

The world of research is very much a world of distributions. Measures have distributions. Statistical tests have distributions. Statistical results have distributions. Even distributions have distributions. Although researchers—and especially statisticians—need to keep them all sorted out, most people do not need to be concerned at that level of detail. Yet even a brief swim in this sea of distributions should be enough to make one a bit wary of the existence of certainty from statistical results.

All of our researchers understand the importance of distributions. All have decided to use statistical techniques that are robust to at least minor violations of normal assumptions. They have dichotomous data for gender. These data form binary distributions because they can take only two values. Additionally, all three researchers know that many of their other measures should at least roughly correspond to the normal curve by the nature of the measure alone, such as height and weight.

Nonetheless, distributions are an area where researchers need to be fairly certain about what they have before generating many complex statistics. Most experienced statisticians graph their data, along with generating some descriptive information, to make an informed decision on whether they have what they think they have. This issue takes judgment, and that judgment often comes from learning from mistakes. Part of the art of research is understanding the subtle relationship between the theoretical distributional underpinnings for a chosen statistic and the distribution presented by the actual data.

After some thought, our researchers believe that they have nominal and ordinal data that do not sufficiently correspond to a normal curve. These data need to be handled differently. Recall that level of measurement determines which statistics are appropriate for data. Nominal and ordinal do not correspond to the normal curve except under special circumstances of dichotomous data, as discussed earlier. Statistics that capitalize on the well-known and quite useful characteristics of the normal curve are called *parametric,* and those that do not (and are appropriate with nominal and ordinal data) are called *nonparametric.* Our researchers are depending upon their consultants for help in this area.

5e.ii. Standard Deviation

The spread of measures
In a normal curve
Yields much information
For analysts to observe

Standard deviations measure the extent of differences in a metric (unit of measurement) that is comparable across measures. They do this by representing placement under the normal curve relative to the center of its bell shape. For IQ, a standard deviation is about 15 points (the mean is about 100). Plus or minus one standard deviation from the mean (in this case, IQs from 85 to 115) will include about 68% of everyone. Plus or minus two standard deviations (IQs from 70 to 130) covers about 95% of everyone under the curve. Plus or minus about three standard deviations (IQs from 55 to 145) includes almost the entire population, about 99.74%. Beyond three standard deviations in either direction on a normal curve, events are rare. With large populations, such as countries, even the tails of the bell-shaped curve (past three standard deviations) can represent large numbers of people. Nonetheless, proportionately, they are still a very small percentage of everyone under consideration, at least under the normal curve.

The size of a standard deviation, relative to its mean, represents the degree of inequality in a characteristic or trait. Relatively wide standard deviations suggest greater inequality for that measure than do relatively small ones. So, standard deviations represent both information content and the degree of inequality in a measure.

If a standard deviation is zero, that measure has no information content in research. For example, if our entire sample is composed of people who are 6 feet tall, testing the impact of height on some other trait cannot be done because there would be no data (and no information content) for other heights; therefore, no frame of reference would exist from which to draw conclusions about the impact of height. The computer would give us an all-but-unintelligible error code, but the result would be the same. No variability means no information content, which means no frame of reference for drawing conclusions.

As measures of inequality, standard deviations can highlight some of the best and worst in society. Importantly, the application of standard deviations to a topic can be subject to personal values. Once more, researchers need to be careful in how they apply their knowledge of the systems and data they have. Showing one group to score lower on a sensitive measure, such as IQ, can spark a debate that is hard to quiet. Various measures show various relationships, whether they fit our sense of civility or not. Researchers need to make personal judgments for where they will and will not be involved. Research is not value free in its application, despite the protests of some who might like to see it otherwise. Questions about gender, race/ethnicity, social status, and many other features of daily life can lead to hurtful results when handled without due concern for topic and context. When researchers make a bomb, they know it might be used. When they drop a few statistics that could be harmful to a particular group, they need to have done so knowingly and reflectively, if at all. The way of research should be to have the debate, while erring on the side of humanity.

Our three researchers are somewhat alike in their understanding and use of standard deviations. They view them as a measure of information content and, more importantly, inequality. Inequality is not a value judgment in this research sense. It is simply a statement of what exists, and it can lead to interesting questions about why the inequalities exist and what might be done to eradicate them.

This point is well worth remembering and sometimes worth debating. Good research is unbiased in terms of personal values, approach, coding, interpretation, and all the small decisions that enter into answering questions. Yet none of us is value free. We are all products of our past, of our pervasive conditioning that permeates all aspects of our conscious lives. To assert that anyone can fully escape this conditioning is to make a classic mistake in research— arrogance. Researchers cannot be fully unbiased. So, although they try to be as unbiased as possible, they must accept the possibility of simply being wrong or unconsciously biased in their approaches. Researchers need to accept these things because human prejudices can influence human results, whether anyone likes it or not. Being constantly aware of these issues helps researchers to keep on the true path of research.

5f. Association

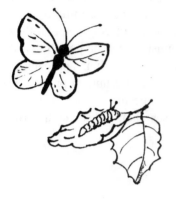

Applied social sciences
Do much with association
Yet thinking too causally
Is a constant temptation

The types of associations covered here are correlations, effect sizes, and coefficients. All three of these measures attempt to inform debates on the degree to which measures seem to be related to other measures. As can be seen from the previous statement, simple association is not so simple after all. The three types of association discussed here are only the beginning of a larger domain of measures of association. Interested researchers should consider exploring some of the more accessible texts on statistics, such as *The Tao of Statistics: A Path to Validity.*

i. Correlation: Correlations are a mathematical method of showing the extent to which two measures move in tandem—whether with each other or in opposite directions.

ii. Effect size: A (somewhat) standardized method of depicting a difference between two groups.

iii. Coefficients: A metric to show the amount of influence that one characteristic has on another.

These three measures of association can actually go a long way toward suggesting causality. Importantly, a temporal element needs to be added to show that one thing happens reliably before the other. Furthermore, the follow-up event should not occur without the causal agent having previously occurred, whenever possible and with notable exceptions.

The entire point of the high school principal's project is to show an association between academic club membership and higher amounts of associated information learned on the subject. He will use all manner of evidence at his disposal to do so. Although researchers are supposed to be unbiased in all regards, he knows that the academic clubs cannot possibly hurt and, logically, should help. With no downside to being wrong, he is willing to be open about his biased perspective to this research. Furthermore, with his stakeholders (e.g., the board of education), he also knows that his enthusiasm is half the battle to achieving reform.

The director of public health is not looking for associations of any kind. She is looking for estimates of vaccine used and destroyed. For her, measures of association belong in some of her other projects.

The professor knows that the heart of qualitative fieldwork can be found in the associations her respondents have with their culture as contrasted with their associations with the other culture. We act and feel differently at home as opposed to abroad. Her mixed methods approach should help her sort out the tenable associations from the less credible information. Nonetheless, her goal is to discount or support a strong association between matrilineal cultures and more equal women's rights, such as a relatively high correlation, discussed next.

5f.i. Correlation

Predicting one from another
Knowing how data relate
When associations are weak
Their value sparks debate

Correlations are much like scores in a pairs synchronized swimming event. The two people involved can achieve perfect scores by identical movements or by exactly opposite movements. Anything in between is not as synchronized. Correlations measure the degree to which values for two measures move in a synchronized manner. The further away from 0 and closer to 1 (moving together) or to −1 (moving opposite each other), the more synchronized they are. The closer to 0, the more independent they are. Generally, correlation values of about +/−0.2 are considered weak, about +/−0.5 are considered moderate, and about +/−0.8 are considered strong. Correlations thus have two aspects: strength and direction. Most of the time, researchers need to know both aspects.

Correlation, by itself, does not imply causation. This point is well worth remembering because it is handled and interpreted incorrectly too frequently to ignore. Correlations assess the strength of mathematical associations. Correlations are not considered to be causal because a different, potentially unmeasured, characteristic might actually be the causal agent. Being human, people state or imply causation more often than they might intend. It is quite easy to slip and state a finding of an association as though it were causal. Many researchers have paid a price in terms of their reputation for implying causation when they had only association.

The high school principal looks at correlations between course grades and many of the other variables. He really wants to understand why the students with the highest grade point averages are not always those who seem the smartest or who do the best on the standardized tests, and he thinks that they might be the ones attending the academic clubs.

The director of public health likes the "mile-high" view that she gets with correlations. She knows that she will need to build quite complex models for many of her questions, especially about the amount of administered vaccine, but simple correlations will help to frame and guide her work.

The professor is searching for strong, positive correlations to support her basic proposition about the relationship between equal rights and matrilineal cultures. Her findings will undoubtedly be complex, and she needs strong correlations to be credible and worthy of additional funding.

5f.ii. Effect Size

A convenient method
From which to assess change
But being "metric free"
Can seem a bit strange

Effect sizes show the impact of a treatment. Functionally, effect sizes can also show the size of the difference between two populations. In either case, the values for the measure are "metric free" by construction. Without going into the required detail, effect sizes are much like means and standard deviations and have their mean value set at "0" and their standard deviation set at "1." With this metric, the average person would have an IQ of zero. A fairly bright person would have an IQ of 1. Relatively few people would have an IQ of 3 or higher, just as very few people would have an IQ lower than −3.

The advantage of effect sizes is in their generalizability across domains and conditions. They are a metric that is easily understood without regard to scaling or the specifics of a given domain. Their interpretation is also easily guided for any conditions that might be locally specific.

Yet for all of their advantages, researchers rarely present effect sizes. Speculating, it might be because there is no "canonized" formula for an effect size. The basic concept is simple . . . the difference in the scores between two groups or a pre- and a posttest is divided by the standard deviation of the population. But that standard deviation can change over time for the same population or could be different for two populations. Especially troublesome about using a "pre" standard deviation is that standard deviations tend to increase over experimental conditions, which would overstate the impact of a treatment. For this reason, some researchers (the authors of this text included) use the mean of the standard deviations for the two groups under consideration as a type of pooled or average measure of the spread of scores.

The high school principal will likely use an outcome of effect sizes in his reports and presentations. That outcome is a percentile movement in the impact of academic clubs. The statement would be something like, "The average student attending an academic club increased academic achievement by 10 percentiles over the average student not attending the clubs. This finding controls for socioeconomic status and prior academic achievement in the topic."

Because the director of public health is looking at a single moment in time and not comparison groups, she has no need for effect sizes for her current project.

The professor is not using data that would lend themselves to effect sizes.

5f.iii. Coefficients

In most complex situations
The number of variables can swell
The importance of each one
Coefficients can tell

Coefficients tell researchers the extent to which one characteristic (or variable) is related to another (or to several others). As such, they are the lifeblood of quantitative research. Yet coefficients are commonly misunderstood. Recall in the sections on error that single numbers most often are really the center of a band of potentially correct results. When they are relatively close to zero for the number of cases being studied, they are said to be functionally zero and are often dropped from equations and ignored.

However, the values for the coefficients were not zero—only statistically indistinguishable from zero. So, some researchers drop the variable and some do not. This issue points to a pair of restrictions from coefficients. First, few reports give enough information about variables that are dropped for a reader to make informed judgments. Because few characteristics are truly independent of other characteristics, dropping variables changes the values of the coefficients that are left in the models, which creates the second restriction—changes in coefficients due to attempts at simplification (referred to as parsimony). Remember that coefficients tell researchers strengths of relationships. When the values for them change according to what is in the equation and what is not, their interpretability is somewhat clouded, which is one of the reasons that strongly worded findings are often suspect.

Samples generate statistics; populations generate parameters. Both of them generate coefficients. Even the mean (i.e., the arithmetic average) is actually a coefficient form of a special case of multiple regression analysis that has been greatly simplified. If the values come from a sample, the coefficients will have error around them, as do all statistics.

Coefficients, then, are technical restrictions because they are presented in a more precise manner than is appropriate to their true interpretation (they could take a range of values), and they often change according to which other variables are in the equation or model.

Our research guides understand the restrictions on their work through the unavoidable use of coefficients in the quantitative aspects of it. They, as with other researchers using quantitative methodologies, have no choice but to generate, assess, report, and discuss coefficients. By reporting in a somewhat humble manner with regard to the strengths of their conclusions, they hope to accommodate the technical restrictions placed on them from coefficients.

5g. Randomness

Maybe here
Maybe there
Maybe anywhere
No why to the where

Randomness is the quality of being unsystematic or haphazard. Characterized as such, randomness becomes an obvious technical restriction because of its lack of predictability. Nonetheless, randomness can also be advantageous.

One area where randomness is a definite advantage is in simple random sampling. Even in its name, simple random sampling depends upon randomness to be the gold standard that it is. Random samples tend to represent their parent groups fairly well, because everyone in the population would have had an equal chance of being included in the sample that is studied. In this sense, randomness means unbiasedness through representativeness.

Yet the restriction from randomness comes from the very characteristic that made it advantageous for sampling—its unpredictability. A large portion of the unpredictability in randomness stems from the error component that is inherent in all of research's measurements. Many researchers handle this issue by being somewhat humble in generalizing their findings, acknowledging that random error could be part of what is leading to their findings and conclusions. They characterize their results and methods as clearly as they can.

Furthermore, open and forthright researchers list all of the limitations of which they are aware. This approach to results presentation is a stellar disposition for how knowledge is best generated.

Our researchers know about the qualities of randomness. They are aware of the advantageous issues related to sampling as well as the disadvantageous issues stemming from a lack of predictability. This almost yin-yang dimension to randomness is a pervasive fact of life in research. In no small way, randomness is the very element that allows both research and statistics to exist. Even so, randomness can, and so often does, greatly complicate research projects, and it requires the assistance of qualified experts to properly characterize it.

5h. Complexity

An explosion of variables
Is complexity's pollution
To move to an answer
Models form the solution

Much of entry-level research methodology is based on theoretical cases with tidy results. The real world is not that way. Every time a researcher turns over a rock, dirt is found—and we need to get it under our fingernails as researchers. Real-life (i.e., applied) research is full of complexities and situations that are not at all similar to those found in textbooks. The reason is that real life is not at all congruent with the assumptions and the conditions upon which research and statistics are presented to students. In applied settings, issues are not independent, and yet independence is an assumption for many statistical and methodological techniques. To add to the complexity—assumptions, which should be requirements for specific methods or techniques, are not always exactly required in their most stringent form. Furthermore, statistics and methodological techniques vary in their ability to return approximately correct values when these assumptions are violated to different degrees. These factors and more can quickly add to the complexity of a research project.

The two complexity issues explored in more depth herein are nested designs and manifest versus latent functions. The reason for highlighting these two facets of complexity is that they tend to confound or undermine a nontrivial proportion of the results reported in research that was conducted by people who do not specialize in conducting research.

  i. Nested designs: when there is a hierarchy in the structure of the data, such as students within courses or schools, which are within a district or state

 ii. Manifest versus latent functions: polity has an intent (manifest), but it also carries with it unintended consequences (latent)

In just about all research, complexity strikes. Research projects tend to go through an inflationary period whereby more and more complexity seems to be added. The reason is that more ideas as to how the system functions get generated. More plausible confounds are introduced and must be accommodated. All manner of explanation can take place, but the result is that the person in charge of the research must work diligently to prevent most research projects from expanding beyond resources' abilities to complete the work. Our research guides understand this situation and use their models to keep their projects focused.

5h.i. Nested Designs

Being within a group
Like being in a bubble
Can create unique conditions
To unravel or face trouble

When situations exist whereby the subjects of an analysis are some-how contained within another group (e.g., patients within doctors, students within specific teachers within courses, or engines within factories), researchers use a nested analysis. Ignoring the nesting has caused almost immeasurable damage to egos and repu-tations, even to science itself. Handling the nesting is often a complex issue, but it should still be done.

The issue is that groups tend to be and to act somewhat more like themselves than do randomly picked individuals from across all groups. Sometimes, that group effect is the target of interest. More often, the apparent nesting becomes a plausible confound that needs to be accommodated in the model one way or another, generally with the help of a qualified statistician or research methodologist.

If there is such a thing (and experience suggests that there might be), the single most likely place that savvy researchers and policymakers start talking past each other (instead of with each other) is when researchers think they are dealing with a nested model with a plausible impact that is too big to be ignored. Both terminology and frustration seem to escalate with incredible speed. Even worse, occupational vocabulary starts to fill the air, further confusing and frustrating half the participants in the now-heated discussion. The lesson to be learned is that complexity can lead to frustration and misunderstanding among professional researchers and lay-people alike.

Our researchers will try to accommodate their nested issues as best they can, with help from the statisticians. The challenge for the statisticians is that no guidelines exist to suggest when the issue is small enough to ignore or large enough that it cannot be safely ignored. Personal judgments are not the same as tradition-ally accepted methodologies for handling situations. This issue leads to one of the largest restrictions in all of research—the appropriate context for the potentially hundreds of often small and undocumented decisions that enter into just about all com-plex research designs, especially when operationalized. Both practitioners and consumers need to be cognizant of these issues. For researchers, it means being somewhat more humble in the strengths of conclusions than would be hoped for a "strong" paper. For consumers of research, this situation means that results should be taken as temporary knowledge that is likely to be refined in the future.

5h.ii. Manifest Versus Latent Functions

Manifest is intended

Latent goes along for the ride

Policy must consider both

Or outcomes can collide

Manifest functions are the intended outcomes of programs or policies. As such, they are the stated goals, missions, and so on of whatever the topic happens to be that is under consideration. The problem comes with the unintended consequences of the programs or policies—the latent functions. Here is an example of how latent functions can work.

Let us assume that the government wanted to encourage people to stop smoking tobacco. The government could criminalize tobacco, but Prohibition taught them that black markets would quickly fill any vacuum in people's wants that is created by governments. Heavy taxes are regressive by falling mainly on those who can least afford them—and really cannot afford tobacco now. So, government could use positive incentives. It could give, say, $1,000 to everyone who stopped smoking. Well, for $1,000, there likely would be plenty of people who would start to smoke, just to be able to claim the money for stopping. Many of these people would become addicted and not be able to stop—more smoking, not less. Alternatively, the government could restrict the monetary incentive to only those people who have smoked at least 5 years. Well, folks smoking 3 or 4 years but considering quitting might wait for their fifth year to be able to collect the money, again further addicting some for life. In this scenario, the unintended functions of a smoking cessation campaign seem to outweigh the intended ones.

For this reason, policies that are quickly developed and implemented often carry unintended consequences. These unintended consequences then require that substantial revisions be made to the policy. In a very real way, bureaucracies can serve populations well by slowing down, debating, and changing policies before they become law.

Our researchers cannot do much about latent functions in their work. They know of them and try to avoid them whenever they can. For example, the high school principal knows that his monitoring of a class meeting fundamentally alters the nature of that class. The director of public health knows that her talking to clinic workers about vaccine destruction might cause them to order less and run short next year. The professor is aware that discussions of women's rights sometimes trigger abusive episodes in relationships with a history of such episodes. All three professionals will try to avoid these types of situations, or at least put them in a proper perspective when they arise, but overall, there is little that can be done to completely eliminate them.

Epilogue

Not all results are published

There are just too many to fit

Many results that are left out

When the analyses are split

The art of the report is the art of audience-specific spin while remaining faithful to the facts. As we emerge on the world of research, we see that order is brought out of chaos, but at a cost. That cost is certainty. Incredibly, the benefit from the loss of total certainty is enormous. Without needing to know how to do many of the more advanced techniques on research, we are now more aware of why and how researchers can be wrong, by not properly heeding the issues associated with research's restrictions. As importantly, we also are more aware of why and how research can be correct, albeit humbly so. To transform this new awareness into an intuitive understanding of patterns and trends that support research as the path to validity requires study, practice, and reflective thought.

Once we internalize the restrictions and see that they can work to our advantage, we see research in a new and uplifting light. Yet our ire can also come out. Reports with divisive conclusions or those written in absolutist terms seem somehow unfair. We want to see the weaknesses of the research made clear. Our ethical standards seem to keep pace with our increasing knowledge of research. We need to be on stronger ground to be assured, or before making statements that could be hurtful to others.

Later, we become more aware of restrictions in reporting as a broader research issue. We might question the specifics of methodologies, statistical techniques, or assumptions of the data. We think of how patterns and trends in the handling of the various issues that can arise can also lead to an almost too convenient set of results.

Eventually, we cannot help but see when findings seem overstated or when assertions do not seem supported by the research. At that moment, we reach a fork in the path of our understanding. Over time, the questions become more complex and about social or other difficult-to-count issues. The number of unknowns in equations increases at a fantastic rate. The push toward parsimony comes under tension from the desire to explain more variation and predict more accurately. Models grow, change, and adapt to changes in theories and advances in the underlying mathematics. Being swept up in this world is what researchers do.

To see the Tao of research in action, watch the faces of researchers when they are becoming successful at weaving together previously unrecognized threads of associations, or when uncovering differences in new and important ways. Knowledge is being born. New questions are being asked and researched. For many researchers, a flash of insight brings a smile across their faces as they see the next steps along their paths and wonder what might lie ahead.

Knowledge is needed

So research is done

Yet of supreme importance

Let the process harm none